THE SWIFTLY TILTING WORLDS OF MADELEINE L'ENGLE

Essays in Her Honor by

E. Beatrice Batson

Barbara Braver

Thomas Cahill

Alzina Stone Dale

Myrna R. Grant

Emilie Griffin

Donald R. Hettinga

Thomas Howard

Calvin Miller

Virginia Stem Owens

Katherine Paterson

Eugene H. Peterson

Robert Siegel

Luci Shaw

Walter Wangerin, Jr.

Walter Wink

The Swiftly Tilting Worlds of

MADELEINE
L'ENGLE

LUCI
SHAW
Editor

Harold Shaw Publishers
Wheaton, Illinois

ISBN 0-87788-483-8

Edited by Luci Shaw

Cover design by David LaPlaca

Library of Congress Cataloging-in-Publication Data

The swiftly tilting worlds of Madeleine L'Engle : essays in her honor
  / edited by Luci Shaw.
    p. cm.
  ISBN 0-87788-483-8
  1. L'Engle, Madeleine—Criticism and interpretation. 2. Christianity and literature—United States—History—20th century. 3. Women and literature—United States—History—20th century. 4. Christian literature, American—History and criticism. I. L'Engle, Madeleine. II. Shaw, Luci.
PS3523.E55Z88 1998
813'.54—dc21
                                            97-49159
                                             CIP

04 03 02 01 00 99 98

10 9 8 7 6 5 4 3 2 1

Contents

Madeleine and I have been friends for close to thirty years. It all started at a Wheaton College Conference on Language and Literature where we exchanged books and began to correspond. Later, I became Madeleine's editor at Harold Shaw Publishers, the company my husband and I initiated, and to date I have worked with Madeleine on eleven books, during which process it became clear that our spirits were knit. We live on opposite coasts of the continent, but our communication is free and frequent. We often travel and vacation together. She has enlarged my world in more ways than I can ever describe.

Madeleine and I both lost our husbands, Hugh and Harold, to cancer in the same year. Over the years and distance our loving friendship has become intentional enough for us to write a book about it—*Friends for the Journey* (Servant, 1997). We also co-authored *WinterSong—Seasonal Readings* (Shaw, 1996).

When the editorial team at Shaw approached me with the idea of putting together a festschrift in honor of Madeleine's eightieth birthday, I thought, "Now *that's* a birthday gift I think Madeleine would like!" And here it is!

Luci Shaw

1

The Partnership of Art & Spirituality

Luci Shaw

In the 1870s Jules Verne, possibly the first sci-fi writer of our contemporary age, wrote his novel *The Desert of Ice*. In the 1970s *The Scientific American* took note of a device employed by Verne to extract his protagonists, a band of Arctic explorers, from a seemingly inextricable dilemma. Their wooden sailing ship had been crushed to splinters in the grip of polar ice, leaving them stranded in the uninhabited and inhospitable reaches of the polar ice cap. To rescue them, and to give his novel a more felicitous ending, Verne tells how these inventive adventurers carved an ice lens from clear ice, through which they focused the sun's rays on pieces of their ship's splintered wood, kindling a life-saving fire that allowed them heat enough to survive until they were rescued. Implausible? *The Scientific American* thought so until its editors successfully managed to duplicate the experiment and kindle a flame using a lens of ice.

When I read the account of this kindling of fire from ice, somehow my imagination was also kindled; the story cried out to me to be written into a poem. Consider the resulting work, "Saved by Optics."

Saved by Optics

First, they must find a chip
  of cold

that has always wanted to see,
to channel the light.

Then, with hands devoid
  of electricity

without matches, even,
and with only splinters
  of strength left

they must carve it out—the rough
eyeball—from under the brow
  of this ice continent

and polish it between
their curved palms' last warmth
into the double convex
  of a lens

a gem without frost, or crack,
cleansed by the flow
  of its own tears.

Next, they must wait, shivering,
for the slow sun
to reach the zenith
  of his readiness

to work with them. Now.
Focused in the eye
  of ice

(angled exactly,
though its chill slows each
  of their fingers' bones)

a matchless flame collects
until the concentrated scrutiny
  of light

reads the dry tinder into
a saving kindling—ice's gift
  of heat, and paradox.[1]

I had felt no compelling theological motivation to write this poem, simply a fascination with an intriguing physical phenomenon. But much later, as I reread the completed poem with a more critical eye (the fires of composition having cooled), I became aware of some correspondences I had not noticed before.

Here was a group of helpless, hopeless human beings in a crisis of existential need, on the verge of extinction in the Arctic freeze, condemned to die by their own inability to create enough warmth to survive. Cold is the antithesis of energy and life, and they were utterly vulnerable to it, their own small internal wick of flame too easily snuffed, their one source of heat being the remote sun, its energy untapped until a creative mind applied a simple principle of physics to the situation. The link between the helpless humans ("without strength" is the biblical phrase that comes to mind) and God, the source of all light, warmth, life, was "a lens," Christ become human, *carved, as it were, from the ice continent itself,* because he had "always wanted" to be a channel for light. Once again the Incarnation is the central theological truth for life. This sinless Christ, "a lens without frost, or crack," his flame "matchless" (the word play also emphasizes the plight of those without matches), was also fully human, weeping for us and with us. Images of cold and heat, light and seeing, pervade the poem, as does the idea of salvation, and grace, appearing in the "gift" of warmth. "Now"—the moment of truth and transformation when the sun's light becomes a searing pinpoint of heat—reminds us of the Scripture's "Now is the accepted time . . . the day of salvation" to be patiently awaited throughout history. In this context the meaning that emerges is that Jesus Christ, God's lens, in whom divine love is uniquely focused, translates the splintered, fragmented tinder of our lives into something of life-enhancing value that can perpetuate the flame, just as the crystalline properties of the ice lens turned the very cause of extinction—cold—into something life-giving for Jules Verne's heroes.

It has been said that faith is "a certain widening of the imagination." When Mary asked the Angel, "How shall these things be?" she was asking God to widen her imagination.

All my life I have been requesting the same thing—a baptized imagination that has a wide enough faith to see the numinous in the ordinary. Without discarding reason, or analysis, what I seek from my Muse, the Holy Spirit, are images that will open up reality and pull me in to its center.

Christian sacramentalism views all of existence as falling under the sovereignty of a beneficent God. The Logos not only spoke the universe into being; he still embraces it, defining and redefining it, assigning it meaning and value at every level. As C. S. Lewis put it: "I believe in Christianity as I believe the sun has risen, not only because I see it but because by it I see everything else."

I seldom sit down to write an explicitly "Christian" poem. But I find that as I allow the created universe and the ingrained Scripture to illuminate me, what I deeply believe pushes up through the fabric of the words, often in surprising and unplanned ways. Usually my compulsion to write comes simply from my own amazement at a striking image. (Poetry is, after all, "the language in which we explore our own amazement," as poet Christopher Fry put it.) But again and again the result suggests how the partnership of art and spirituality probes the meaning that lies beneath the surface of all phenomena, waiting to be recognized and acknowledged. And this is, of course, the benison of the sacramental view of life, in which everything points to something, and everything has meaning. As Flannery O'Connor put it, "The writer who is thoroughly Christian will be unable to write anything without in some way revealing God."

I suspect that my topic, "The Partnership of Art & Spirituality," needs some definitions if we are to see the connection of these two related but distinct modes of seeing and expression within the same framework of understanding, and together celebrate their marriage.

For me, art is the impulse that gathers materials from our disparate and fragmented, but rich and compellingly diverse universe and assembles them in a way that brings a kind of order out of their chaos, an order with elements of both conflict and resolution. Art is also the result of our human impulse to find expression for that "something" within us which responds to stimuli around us and cries out to be expressed, to find a meaning in beauty or terror or conflict or sex or in something as mundane as food, and to reflect this in a form that produces a response—awe, excitement, disgust, wonder, even anger—in those around us.

This aesthetic impulse seems to be universal. Art finds meaning in all of human experience or endeavor, drawing from it strength and surprise by reminding us of what we know but have never before truly seen, transcending our particularity with soaring ease. There is no society on earth that does not attempt to decorate or embellish or enhance its dwelling places or garments or artifacts or the human body itself with graphic design or fabric or song or word or ritual. Just consider the act of getting dressed for the day, your getting dressed for this day, and realize what delicate and calculated decisions were required for you to present yourself in public. It is not enough for us to be warm, and decent. We aim to attract and impress as well! But art goes beyond attractiveness. It takes off the clothes of the world and revels in the body beneath and sooner or later sells tickets so that we can all enter the exhibit. Maybe art and religion are aligned because religion also undresses the world in its attempt to seek and find, knocking, and trusting that God will open a door.

Art lays bare our realities, and religion opens up experience to the gaze of God. Think of the wonderful iconography of the Greek and Russian Orthodox communities. Think of the way native American art and animistic African art mirror their belief systems. And church structure, with its cross-shaped nave and transept, its wealth of sign and symbol and story in stained glass, stone and wood carving. Consider the very design of the church building itself, which was called, in preliterate societies, "the poor man's Bible" because it filled the heart and mind with images and colors and shapes which spoke of divine realities. Art was seen in medieval and renaissance painting and sculpture and music as a vehicle for expressing the glory of God. In the Baroque era composers such as Bach made notations on their musical scores: *Soli gloria deo*—"glory to God alone." Art and spirituality were true partners.

With the Enlightenment, art and religion began to split apart in European and Western culture, so that even a poet as deeply in tune with the natural and supernatural worlds as Gerard Manley Hopkins felt compelled to burn his early work—a sacrifice he labeled "the slaughter of the innocents." For seven years Hopkins rigorously disciplined himself, attempting in his priestly role to worship and serve God apart from poetry, until his religious superior hinted that "someone" ought to write a poem about the wreck of the ship the *Deutschland* . . . a comment which spurred Hopkins's poetic career anew.

In our created universe pure functionality might have seemed to be enough. How essential—we might ask—is beauty for the working of the universe? Philosophers and metaphysicians may disagree in their answers, and, surprisingly, "elegance" is something that today's scientists strive for in their theories and equations. For me, it seems that the inclusion of the desire and appreciation for the beautiful is gratuitous—an infusion of pure Grace, a reflection of the heart of the Creator. When we create something appealing, even in acts as mundane as arranging our living rooms and choosing the color of the wallpaper or choosing a typeface from our printer fonts, we show our integral relationship with the Creator. God—the first Quilter of prairies, the prime Painter (sunsets, night skies, forget-me-nots, thunderheads), the archetypal metal Sculptor (mountain ranges, the crystalline structure of metals and gemstones), the Composer who heard bird songs and the whales' strange, sonorous clickings and croonings in his head long before there were birds or whales to sing them, the Poet whose Word was "full of grace and truth"—in that divine image we humans are made, participating in creative intelligence and originality with its essential beauty. As Frederick Buechner says: "Beauty is to the spirit what food is to the flesh. It fills an emptiness in you which nothing else can fill."

Art often speaks to us *subliminally,* sub-liminally, "below the threshold" of our conscious awareness. *Limen* is Latin for threshold and is often applied in connection with the kind of knowledge that comes to us in ways that bypass both our cognitive reasoning and our senses. In that regard, art—poetry, music, painting, dance—helps us to see the unseeable and know the unknowable, ushering us into the realm of the transcendent. Imagination, which is spirituality's companion, is the window to the soul/spirit. It is the capacity programmed into us to see pictures in our heads. As Dorothy Sayers says: "We see the Creed as a series of pictures." Imagination, and metaphor, the making of truth or story into verbal pictures rather than propositional prose statements, is the methodology consistently called upon in the imagery of Scripture—the teaching tool on which God seems to have set the imprint of his approval by constant use.

One-third of Scripture is poetry, and a great deal of its prose is salted with vivid imagery. Rather than teach or correct only through abstractions or doctrinal statements, the Bible *shows us* through myth, story, parable, vision, poetry, illustration, dream, analogical and anagogical imagery—all of which open us up to understanding and meaning. And imagery does not need to be explained. Its content is felt or experienced imaginatively. An image prints itself on the mind, and sometime, perhaps years, later a spiritual connection is made. As Emily Dickinson put it: "The truth must dazzle gradually." In his poem "The Poet as a Window," George Herbert also showed God's high regard for imagery as a way of teaching:

Lord, how can man preach thy eternall word?
* He is a brittle crazie glasse:*
Yet in thy temple thou dost him afford
* This glorious and transcendent place,*
* To be a window, through thy grace.*

Doctrine and life, colours and light, in one
* When they combine and mingle, bring*
A strong regard and awe . . . [2]

We are astonished at the way the link between the visible

and invisible worlds is made. Faith is not linear. It is, indeed, a widening of the imagination, a leap into the transcendent, a taste of the numinous, a vision of the extraordinary in the ordinary. And our coach for the leap, the glue in the link, is our Muse, the Spirit of God.

A phenomenal resource—the Spirit. As Christians and artists we are not just followers, plodding imitators, or self-propelled innovators. We are empowered from within our own imaginations by the First Poet, the Primal Artist, the Original Composer. Our own creative spirits, made in the image of Another, are boosted and blessed and set on fire by our union with God in Christ.

There is a radical nature to both art and faith. Both are epiphanic—"manifestations." Both are transformative; we are changed as we enter their gleaming realms. They are full of inexplicable transitions and showings, mysterious both in their origin and in their mechanism.

Does art influence spirituality? Does our spirituality affect our art? Yes. And yes. The two seem symbiotic, each feeding on and nourishing the other. They work in tandem. It is hard to imagine an artist who is totally unspiritual, in the sense of being out of touch with both created and unseen worlds. And it is hard to imagine a person full of the Spirit who is not in some way creative, innovative, world-disturbing.

Fullness of life in both arenas—art and spirituality—demands that we let go, that we relinquish control—something that goes against the human grain, particularly in a culture obsessed with empowerment. Here we are, trying to bring order and beauty out of chaos, to gain a species of control, to exercise the authority of experience and wisdom, and we have to let go again? How seemingly counterproductive. But it is in both accepting and using the gift, and the giving it back, that we find the rounding out of the process, the completion, the deepest fulfillment. We have to give of ourselves to art, but we have to accept that what we give is never enough, that for eternal significance any art, literature, music, drama must be Spirit-driven, Spirit-imprinted.

Walter Brueggemann tells us that poetry is needed to "disclose" truths that are "closed" by prose:

> Our technical way of thinking reduces mystery to problem, transforms assurance to rigid certitude, revises quality into quantity, and so takes the categories of biblical faith and represents them in manageable shapes. . . .There is then no danger, no energy, no possibility, no opening for newness . . . truth is greatly reduced. To address the issue of a truth greatly reduced requires us to be poets who speak against a prose world.[3]

So, for Brueggemann, art allows us to oppose the false clarity of oversimplification and to disclose the truth in its diverse richness and complexity, and its subtle nuance, making it perhaps less manageable, but no less true.

In the context of control and manageability, the word *surrender* comes to mind—a word with somewhat negative connotations for me. It speaks too loudly of the sawdust trail, the guilt-charged evangelistic meetings of my youth. My word of choice is *abandon,* a wild and wanton word whose noun form is as powerful to me as its verb form.

Madeleine L'Engle has said that "to be an artist means to approach the light, and that means to let go our control, to allow our whole selves to be placed with absolute faith in that which is greater than we are."[4] And when God created us with free wills, he let go of his control. He relinquished both the power and the glory of heaven. But you know that story . . .

Back to definitions. What do we mean by spirituality? In the conservative British evangelical circles in which I grew up, a fellow Christian might have been described as being "spiritually on fire," or "spiritually alive," a phrase which referred to a devout, "sold-out," committed Christian. The crucial question on which one's reputation hung in those circles was: "Is he or she *interested in spiritual things?*" (instead of simply following the Christian patterns of behavior).

Today the term has a far broader scope and hazier edges, often without a specifically religious connotation. Someone described as spiritual is thought to be in touch with the non-material, transcendent world of ideas and emotions; to be "sensitive," open-minded, as much attuned to the soul as to the body. Under the nomenclature of spirituality we have not only the concern of Christians who wish to live out their faith, but also those who seek an eclectic mix of notions that suit their individual religious eccentricities. The massage therapist I sometimes visit describes herself as spiritual; so do my psychotherapist and the young man who does my hair. I have a Siamese cat whose silent, mysterious comings and goings, and whose penetrating sapphire gaze might qualify him as spiritual by this contemporary definition; he goes on *retreat,* for goodness' sake, spending much of his first week with us holed up behind the Bible commentaries in my bookcase—a "spiritual" cat.

This aspect of spirituality partakes more of that characteristic described by the French as *spirituelle* than what is for me a more central description—that Christian spirituality which is rooted in Christ and mediated by Christ's Spirit. We come to the understanding and practice of spirituality mainly by way of revelation—through the primary revelations—the biblical Scriptures and the Christ of Scripture, which are often linked, for me, with the "second Bible" of the natural universe, with its clues and hints to God's creatorship.

On the other hand, my spiritual director, a wonderfully fresh, earthy, intuitive, biblically literate Roman

Catholic woman, is one of the people with whom the word *spiritual* fits most definitely and appropriately—to be with her is to be in Christ's presence. It also fits my son John, a doctor-poet and tropical disease specialist in Africa, who has been a kindred spirit and fellow pilgrim with me most of his life. Today our investigation of the ways of God takes place mostly by e-mail and fax; spirituality is not necessarily technophobic!

The trouble with all this defining and redefining is that the word *spirituality* becomes so broadly defined as to be almost emptied of significance. It can mean whatever we want it to mean. But the persistence of spiritual hunger and thirst—those seasons of drought and rain in poetry, in California weather, and in spiritual vitality—or a sense of connection with God, the transcendent Almighty, in the context of an overwhelmingly material universe is a kind of evidence of its existence and importance. In C. S. Lewis's words: "If I find in myself a desire which no experience in this world can satisfy, the most probable explanation is that I was made for another world." Spirituality and spiritual reality do not lend themselves to physical analysis, nor are they susceptible to rational proof. But neither can they be denied. And though invisible, their very invisibility is a challenge that makes us want them more, and draws us out in the strenuous effort of question and search.

But in this, spirituality is very like the creative impulse towards art—often fickle and unpredictable. We have an untamable, undomesticated God (whom we tend to trivialize to make us feel safe), and the artistic and spiritual gifts from this Creator's hand are not to be summoned with a flick of the wrist or a pleading tone of voice.

Listen to Annie Dillard:

Let us . . . consider, just consider, that the weft of materials admits of a very few, faint, unlikely gaps.

People are, after all, still disappearing, still roping robes on themselves, still braving the work of prayer, insisting they hear something, even fighting and still dying for it. The impulse to a spiritual view persists, and the evidence of that view's power among historical forces and among contemporary ideas persists, and the claim of reasoning men and women that they know God from experience persists.[5]

This mystery, this spill of clues to an unseen reality, is very much a part of the artist's as well as the mystic's life. I wait in silence, by the sea or in the woods or in the deep silence of two o'clock in the morning when I can't sleep, or, more likely, in the press of a desk overflowing with other people's urgencies, for a poem to call me, to claim me, to write *me,* much as I wait, in prayer, for my God to speak, to respond, to direct, or to correct me. I am not in control. I cannot turn on poetry or transcendence as I turn on a faucet. My job is to wait and see—literally, to *wait,* and to *see.* And then, like the aging apostle John on Patmos, to heed the injunction to "fear not," but to "write what I see."[6] And it is the eyes of the imagination, widened by faith, which see, and which please Christ. "Blessed are your eyes, for they see," Christ said, "and your ears, for they hear."[7]

In this waiting time I must be sure that my antennae are out, tasting the air, ready to pull in the messages. Receptivity, yes. Waiting, yes. Active readiness, yes. For passivity has no place in the life of art or Christian spirituality. Art and spirituality are not conveniences, nor do they call to us at convenient times. A poem will begin in my head as I prepare a dinner for eight, at which point I am likely to turn absent-minded, to break an egg into the garbage disposal or put the pot of hot coffee in the refrigerator. God's Spirit will call me to prayer or meditation as I am paying my bills or shopping in the supermarket. Or my mind will catch one idea after another all night long (when I really need the sleep); at such times I am grateful for the collection-jar of my computer monitor glowing in the dark, ready to catch and hold those unanticipated, uninvited lightning bugs of ideas for the morning. And in that morning I am so energized by all this magnetizing activity that I do not feel the lack of sleep! As Dorothy Sayers has her heroine Harriet Vane say at the completion of a sonnet, "I feel like God on the Seventh Day!"[8]

While I was still a student at Wheaton College, studying English literature, the teacher who later became my mentor and dear friend, Clyde Kilby, gave me a small paperback book titled *The Creative Process*. It was a collection of essays by phenomenally gifted people in a number of disciplines—astronomy, molecular biology, sculpture, philosophy, architecture, mathematics, and, of course, fiction and poetry. What they all had in common, expressed in letters or journal entries or lectures, was their sense that their seminal ideas, the images and concepts which were foundational to their most important contributions to science or philosophy or literature or art, were given them from somewhere outside, beyond them. As the poet Stephen Spender expressed it in that very anthology, "My alpha-plus ideas arrived from God-knows-where—quite literally." We are all familiar with C. S. Lewis's account of how the Narnian Chronicles came into being. Lewis remembered: "As with the Ransom stories [his Space Trilogy], the Narnian tales began with *seeing pictures in my head. The Lion, the Witch, and the Wardrobe* all began with a picture of a faun carrying an umbrella and parcels in a snowy wood." Like a dream, this image appeared from nowhere, demanding that Lewis enflesh it in a story. But, of course, it did not come from *nowhere.*

How does my art affect my spirituality? In my journal, art and spirituality are almost a single stream. I write in

it whatever is going on internally at a given moment—
the seed image of a poem or its early stages of growth,
a prayer for help, the connection between an incident
and an idea, a sign of God's love in my life, an idea for
an article, the puzzle of priorities, a feeling of gratitude
or despair or exhilaration . . . it is all there, and it is
hard for me to divide out what is art, what is spirituality,
what is literary, what is merely human. All I know is that
as I place myself in God's hands, he superintends and
guides it all in a way so remarkable that it cannot be
coincidence.

This is the way the Muse moves—mysterious as a
ghost. I conclude with a poem about that mysterious
and holy ghost:

Ghostly

I think often about the invisible
God—doubly covert. I mean, now and
     again
Father and Son made their appearances,
speaking bold in thunder, blood,
or salvation. But the Third
Person is a ghost. Sometimes
he silvers for a moment, a moon sliver
between moving leaves. We aren't sure.

What to make of this . . . How
to see breath? As energy
hovering, birdlike, over chaos,
breeding it into ferns and whales;
blessing the scalps of the righteous
with a pungency of oil; bleeding the hard
edge of warning into all those
prophet voices; etching
Ezekiel's view with oddities—
eyes in wheels spinning like astrolabes;

crowding Mary's womb to seed its
dark clay; wising up fools to improbable
truth; filling us like wine bottles;
bursting from our mouths in champagne
    gasps
of surprise? This for sure—he finds
enough masks to keep us guessing:
Is it really you? Is this you also?

It's a cracked, crossover world, waiting
for bridges. He escapes our categories,
choosing his shapes—fire, dove,
wind, water, oil—closing the breach
in figures that flicker within
the closed eye, tongue the brain, sting
and tutor the soul. Once incarnate
in Judaea, now he is present
(in us in the present
tense), occupying our bodies—
shapes to be reshaped—
houses for this holy ghost. In our special
flesh he thrives into something
too frequent to deny, too real to see.[9]

Author Biography

Luci Shaw, co-founder and past president of Harold Shaw Publishers, has been writer in residence at Regent College, Vancouver, Canada, since 1988. She is author of seven volumes of poetry, including *Polishing the Petoskey Stone* (Shaw, 1990) and *Writing the River* (Piñon Press, 1994), has edited three poetry anthologies, and has written several prose books, the most recent being *Water My Soul: Cultivating the Interior Life with God* (Zondervan). She has also co-authored

two books with Madeleine L'Engle, the most recent being *Friends for the Journey* (Servant). She
lectures widely in North America and abroad on
topics such as art and spirituality, the poetic
imagination, and journal-writing as an aid to
artistic growth. A member of the Chrysostom
Society, she lives with her husband, John Hoyte,
in Bellingham, Washington.

When I wanted to write about the Bible's "Principalities and Powers," Madeleine L'Engle's trilogy was the deepest work I could find on the subject, even though it was fiction. So I called her up, and she had my wife and me over for dinner. Turns out she had read some of *my* stuff on the subject.

Walter Wink

2
Evil in *The Wind in the Door*

Walter Wink

The book awards went to *A Wrinkle in Time* and *A Swiftly Tilting Planet,* but my award goes to the middle volume of Madeleine L'Engle's "children's" trilogy, *A Wind in the Door.* To recap, *Echthroi* (the Greek word for "enemy") are Xing away whole chunks of the universe. Meg is permitted to glimpse this destruction:

> She stood beside him [Progo, her helping cherubim, whose name in Greek means "Foreknowledge"], looking at the brilliance of the stars. Then came a sound, a sound which was above sound, beyond sound, a violent, silent, electrical report, which made her press her hands in pain against her ears. Across the sky, where the stars were clustered as thickly as in the Milky Way, a crack shivered, slivered, became a line of nothingness. . . .
> "Progo, what is it? What happened?"
> "The Echthroi have Xed."
> "What?"
> "Annihilated. Negated. Extinguished. Xed."
> Meg stared in horrible fascination at the rent in the sky. This was the most terrible thing she had ever

seen . . . She pressed close to the cherubim, surrounding herself with wings and puffs of smoke, but she could still see the rip in the sky. She could not bear it.

Meg asks the cherubim, "How—oh, Progo, how did the Echthroi do that?" He responds,

It has to do with un-Naming. If we are Namers, the Echthroi are un-Namers, non-namers. . . . I think your mythology would call them fallen angels. War and hate are their business, and one of their chief weapons is un-Naming—making people not know who they are. If someone knows who he is, really knows, then he doesn't need to hate. That's why we still need Namers, because there are places throughout the universe like your planet Earth. When everyone is really and truly Named, then the Echthroi will be vanquished. . . . There is war in heaven, and we need all the help we can get. The Echthroi are spreading through the universe. Every time a star goes out another Echthros has won a battle. A star or a child or a farandola—size doesn't matter, Meg. The Echthroi are after Charles Wallace [her brother] and the balance of the entire universe can be altered by the outcome.

Many fantasy stories feature an apocalyptic war between good and evil forces. What sets L'Engle and Tolkien apart is their insight that evil cannot be overcome *out there* in the evil beings, but first and most profoundly must be faced in one's own heart. From *Star Wars* to the Power Rangers, the dominant cultural theme is overcoming evil through violence, through destroying its bearers—violence in the service of good is good. But what masters of wisdom like L'Engle teach us is that the very sight of evil engenders evil in our own hearts. To see evil is to wish to destroy it, by whatever means. Violence always appears quickest. And so we are made over into the very evil we hate. Our hate makes us mirror the evil we would eradicate. We want to X it, and in so doing, we in turn become Echthroi.

Meg's first instinct is to hate the evil she encounters. First she must deal with the weak and incompetent Mr. Jenkins, the primary school principal. Her very hatred opens Mr. Jenkins to being possessed by the Echthroi. But not completely possessed; he had shown compassion to Meg's boyfriend once by buying him a new pair of shoes. He cannot be as bad as Meg believes. So the Echthroi can only make doubles of him. One of the cleverest sections of the book involves Meg's having to discern which of the three Mr. Jenkinses is the real one. She can only do so by Naming the correct one, but Naming requires loving, and Mr. Jenkins is precisely the last person in her world she could love. Finally, she sees Mr. Jenkins's few good points. Then she faces her own culpability in fouling their relationship. But the way L'Engle brings her to the breakthrough of loving is magic, and, to my mind, utterly believable.

In the final analysis, love is the greatest exorcist. With love, Meg can now name the real Mr. Jenkins; the impostor Mr. Jenkinses depart with a great howling and shrieking and slashing of the air. The first test has been passed, and now Mr. Jenkins, for some strange reason, has become a companion and a necessary ally.

The problem is that the Echthroi have found a way into Meg's brother, Charles Wallace, by means of the farandolae that make up his mitochondria. Millions of years ago these mitochondria probably swam into what eventually became our eukaryotic cells and just stayed there. They are quite separate from us, having their own DNA and RNA, yet they are symbiotic with us. We are completely dependent on them for our oxygen. And these mitochondria in turn, says L'Engle (leaving behind firm science for free fantasy), are made up of farandolae so tiny that they are invisible even to an electron microscope. The Echthroi have persuaded the junior farandolae not to Deepen, but rather to place themselves at the center of the universe. This inflated self-estimation is especially absurd for farandolae, which are so infinitesimally small, but the situation for human beings is no different, given the proportions of human being versus the vastness of interstellar space. By refusing to Deepen, the farandolae are altering the balance; the song they sing will be stilled, and Charles Wallace will die. It makes no difference how small or how large the rebellious creature is: yielding to the Echthroi has cosmic implications.

I am reminded here of Gandhi, whose commitment to truth and justice was so profound that he would go anywhere and would support any group who had right on their side. And he was prepared to die for even the smallest cause. This is in profound contrast to most of us, who might at a stretch be willing to lay down our lives for a sensational cause sure to hit television news worldwide! What could the opposition do against Gandhi? They could not refute his moral judgment, but they were prepared to ignore it. What they could not ignore was his moral courage, which led him to risk fasting to death simply to set things right. In the face of such overwhelming moral rectitude, they withered.

In the same way, L'Engle sees the survival of the smallest child (in this case, Charles Wallace) as having repercussions for the entire universe. Any victory over the Echthroi that have cast a shadow over our planet is a victory for the universe, and every loss, a tragedy that affects the farthest galaxy. Every star has been Named, every child, every mitochondrion, even every farandola.

But overcoming the Echthroi, if it is to be done without violence (that is, without becoming mirror images of the Echthroi), requires just such willingness to sacrifice as Gandhi manifested. At one point, Progo faces the choice between being Xed by the Echthroi, and Xing himself. At the end, to save Meg, he does X himself, as an act not of suicide, but of redemptive sacrifice. At another juncture, young farandolae tickle an Echthros who is pretending to be Mr. Jenkins until he lets go his prey. They pay with their lives. Repeatedly Meg and Calvin and finally even Mr. Jenkins risk their survival to save their companions and the object of all their concern, Charles Wallace. Again, it is love that overcomes evil, sacrificial love that overcomes *even our hatred of the evil we oppose.* No task could be harder for a human being, for whom justice is often synonymous with revenge. To be able to oppose evil with every fiber of our beings, and at the same time love it unconditionally, is well beyond our human capacity. Time after time, Progo the cherubim enfolds Meg in his wings or sends her life energy or extricates her from the clutches of the Echthroi. This delightful being is L'Engle's down-to-earth personification of what theologians call divine grace. But as a novelist, L'Engle is too shrewd to use theological shortcuts and cliches, however venerable and true. Even God is barely mentioned in this volume, and then as an ambiguous "he" or "the Glory." L'Engle loves the angels and moves among them like an old familiar, wisecracking with beings of unutterable wonder.

The end comes finally when Meg, hearing Mr. Jenkins squeak out, "Nature abhors a vacuum," embraces all of her friends, and even the Echthroi:

Echthroi! You are Named! My arms surround you. You are no longer nothing. You are. You are filled. You are me.
You are
Meg.

Here the gesture is everything. Hatred of evil gives evil life, energy, definition. It is We against They. Good against evil. Life against Death. It all sounds so moral, so conscientious, so virtuous. But it is the way of the Echthroi, who are never more devious than when they persuade us to be righteous in our outrage against evil. The gesture is hands braced in front of us, fighting against evil with all our might, but fighting it *on its own terms,* becoming inexorably like the very thing we oppose.

Meg's is the way of embrace. It absorbs the evil. It breaks the spiral of violence by interposing its own body, self, being. It involves the painful, death-like facing of the evil *in ourselves.* It strips from us the mantle of righteousness, and exposes us as no different in kind from the evil we want so badly to believe is outside us. It humiliates us into a blessed smallness, in which we become far too small to fight against evil all alone, and gently lowers us into the wings of the cherubim, and fills us with the song of the universe, and retunes us to the harmony of the Whole.

I am continually amazed by the fact that the four forces of the universe—the strong force, the weak force, the gravitational force, and the electromagnetic force—all operate by attraction. The universe does not so much enforce its laws as let us break ourselves on them. When we pollute the water, the planet does not strike out at us with lightning. It merely waits, for sooner or later we will have to drink that water. Indeed, attraction is nothing other, emotionally speaking, than love. The power of the universe is love. It lures, it persuades, it entices by its unutterable beauty, its attractive summons. When the cherubim Name that power, they call it Love (or Luff, on Provo's first try).

Love's costly embrace of evil also prevents some tragic mistakes. Most of us are quite sure that we know evil when we see it. But in fact, what we call evil may be someone else's good. Or what we call evil appears so now but later, in light of subsequent events, proves beneficial. Or our calling something evil is contaminated by prejudice, bias, ignorance, misinformation, propaganda, ideology, socialization, and so forth.

When we try to destroy evil, therefore, we risk destroying what is from other, possibly superior, viewpoints, good. When we embrace the evil, we avoid that risk by holding it to us until it, or we, or both together, change. We overcome our homophobia. We see through the lies of a propaganda campaign. We recognize our racism, our ethnocentrism, our limited perspectives. We meet people we had once feared and learn to love them. We get better information. We outgrow our parents' skewed perspectives. And because we have held our enemies to our hearts rather than driving them away, we are wonderfully positioned for forgiveness, reconciliation, and new relationships.

Madeleine L'Engle is a very rare human being in our society. She takes evil seriously. She has a family friend of Meg's say, "That stuff about cosmic screams and rips in distant galaxies offends every bit of the rational part of me." And Meg herself says, "I hoped maybe we could ignore it. Like ostriches or something." All of us would like to do so. Most succeed. Our materialist worldview leads us to explain apparent evil as chance, ignorance, or merely the indifference of a mindless universe.

L'Engle has a different take. One of her characters insists, "There are evil forces at work in the world. . . . They are throughout the universe. . . . They are the powers of nothingness, those who would un-Name. Their aim is total X—to extinguish all creation." In a universe in which freedom, mind, and at least rudimentary choice go "all the way down," as the process philosophers like to put it, then wrong choice, uncreative choice, destructive choice goes all the way down as well. So it may be simply one more anthropocentric illusion that only human beings are capable of evil. Look at disease germs and viruses. L'Engle's Echthroi are just the kind of being-devourers that the misuse of freedom would postulate. Christian tradition called them "fallen angels." What L'Engle has accomplished is to take that virtually unintelligible language of the past and pour into it an astonishing new vitality.

There is an unresolved riddle that L'Engle does not attempt to address but which tantalizes me. When at the end Meg embraces and absorbs the Echthroi, they cannot have come into her in their evilness. They had to have been transformed. Does that not suggest that the fallen Powers can be redeemed, however malignant? That these Powers can be restored to the Harmony, re-learn the song, and sustain those lives whose well-being they were created to serve? If loving our enemies is the ultimate sacrifice of love, then is it not true that love can never leave its enemies to their just destruction, but must struggle through to that ultimate embrace, the end of the world, the restitution of all things? I wonder what Madeleine would say.

I have written a half dozen theological works on the Powers That Be that, taken together, do not add up to a fraction of the wisdom in this book. And I will never know how much my own work on the Powers lies under obligation to Madeleine's trilogy, which I long ago read aloud to my children, acutely aware that its characters might be children, but its message demands an adult maturity that few of us possess.

Author Biography

Dr. Walter Wink is professor of biblical interpretation at Auburn Theological Seminary in New York City. Previously, he was a parish minister and taught at Union Theological Seminary in New York City. In 1989-1990 he was a Peace Fellow at the United States Institute of Peace.

He is author of a trilogy, *Naming the Powers:*

The Language of Power in the New Testament, Unmasking the Powers: The Invisible Forces That Determine Human Existence, and *Engaging the Powers: Discernment and Resistance in a World of Domination* (Fortress Press). The third volume, *Engaging the Powers,* received three Religious Book of the Year awards for 1993, from Pax Christi, the Academy of Parish Clergy, and the Midwestern Independent Publishers Association. Among his other recent works are *The Powers That Be* (Doubleday, 1998) and *Healing a Nation's Wounds: Reconciliation on the Road to Democracy* (Life and Peace Institute, 1997).

Like so many others, I first met Madeleine L'Engle through her books, which are nourishment indeed. Few books I have read have made so deep an impression on me as *A Wrinkle in Time*. When I invited her to give a homily during an advent vespers series that I had organized at Saint Joseph's Church in Greenwich Village, she accepted, and the evening of her homily my wife, Susan, and I had the immense pleasure of meeting Madeleine and her extraordinary husband, Hugh Franklin. That was almost fifteen years ago.

Since then my admiration for this remarkable woman has grown into an oak tree of wonder. I have watched her dispense anonymous generosity to those in need and have known her to forgive and forget with a style so graceful that few, if any, could match it. My family and I have been recipients of the grace that flows through Madeleine, so I know most personally whereof I speak.

In what follows, "Saint Patrick's Message for Us," I would like to return homily for homily. Those who know Madeleine will notice the echoes of her in this evocation of the distant past. Like Saint Patrick, she has an uncanny ability to see things as if no one has ever seen them before; like him, she has suffered green-eyed opposition from those who are always sure they are right; like him, she relies on the oceanic mercy of God. Like Saint Brigid, her hospitality is legendary, her arms open wide to receive the least of the brothers and sisters of Jesus, and there radiates from her person that effortless nobility of spirit that is impossible to fake.

Thomas Cahill

3
Saint Patrick's Message for Us*

Thomas Cahill

Saint Patrick was not born with the word *saint* in front of his name. To the people of his own time—some 1500 years ago—he did not look like a saint. He looked like an ordinary human being, like the person sitting next to you or in front of you or behind you, maybe even like you. And in his own time, many people did not believe he was a saint at all—and they said so. They gossiped about him behind his back; they accused him of being a phony; they said he was up to no good.

This was all because Patrick was a revolutionary. He thought something no one had ever thought before: he thought the Irish were human. Nice people—people with nice houses and nice bank accounts and nice educations and nice manners—did not want anything to do with the Irish. All the nice people were called Romans. In those days, wherever you lived—in Europe or Africa or even as far away as the island of Britain—if you were a nice person, you were a Roman citizen. If you were not a nice person—if you lived in a hut or stole cattle for a living or painted your face blue and dressed funny (or sometimes did not dress at all but charged around in your birthday suit)—you were a barbarian. The Irish were barbarians; so were the Scots and the Picts, the Germans and the Scandinavians; so were most of the Slavs and many of the Africans. But the Irish were the worst barbarians of all; they were always fighting one another; in fact, they were such fierce warriors that the Romans decided not to bother to conquer them. The Irish practiced human sacrifice; they offered up newborn babies to the harvest gods and prisoners of war to the war gods. They specialized in kidnapping Roman children, whom they would then sell into slavery.

In one of these Irish kidnapping raids on the west coast of Roman Britain, Patrick was captured. He was then not a saint at all: he was a Roman teenager; and he tells us that he thought he was pretty hot stuff. He knew, for instance, that his parents were idiots: for one thing, they worked hard; and, for another thing, they believed in God. Patrick did not know what he wanted to be, but he knew he did not want to be like his parents.

But then he was captured by Irish pirates, who put him in chains and sailed back to Ireland and forced him to be a slave among the Irish barbarians, who treated him barbarously. He tells us he never had enough to eat; he did not even have clothes to wear: he went hungry and naked. He had no one to turn to. He began to pray. He prayed in secret, when no one could hear him, while he was shepherding sheep on the cold, damp mountains of Antrim in Northern Ireland. He prayed for six years, from the time he was sixteen to the time he was twenty-two. And then one night, while he was sleeping, Patrick heard a voice. The voice said: "Your hungers are rewarded; your sufferings are at an end. You are going home." Patrick sat up and looked around and realized that the Voice was coming not from outside him but from inside him. The Voice continued: "Look, your ship is ready."

Patrick was nowhere near the sea, but he got up and walked 200 miles to an inlet on the east coast of Ireland. There he saw his ship. He jumped on board, and it set sail. He was free at last.

Patrick knew now that he was under the protection of a good God, the same God who had made the mountains and the sea and you and me and Patrick himself, the same God who loves human beings so much that he was willing to make the ultimate sacrifice: "For God so loved the world that he gave his only begotten Son" to die for our sake. At last, the Voice that spoke within Patrick identified itself, saying: "He who gave his life for you, he it is who speaks within you."

The Voice told Patrick to go back to Ireland, to return to the people who had treated him so badly, to bring them the gospel, the Good News that Jesus had died for each of them, that they were forgiven every horrible thing they had ever done, that God loved them—more spectacularly than all their wars, more scandalously than all their sacrifices—that God loved them with a fierce, undying love.

Patrick went. He did the unthinkable. Patrick went. He returned to the land of his captivity, to the land of the terrifying Irish. Patrick went. He brought the gospel with him. He told the Irish that they no longer had to offer human sacrifice, that Christ had died once for all, that God was not evil like them but good—and did not want blood sacrifice. He told them that even they were not as evil as they thought they were: they were children of God, his handiwork. If their sins were scarlet, they would be made white as snow. For "all the wickedness in this world that man might do or think / Is no more to the mercy of God than a live coal in the sea." He taught them to call this God their father, to hallow his

39

name and ask for his protection, which in his fatherly love he would not refuse.

And the Irish listened to Patrick. They threw away their knives of sacrifice and overturned their monstrous altars. They made new rules for warfare, which made wars smaller, less frequent, and less bloody. The pirate ships sat in the harbors, and the Irish slave trade came to an end.

The Irish took to the gospel with the same gusto with which they had gone to war. Just as they had been the world's most terrifying warriors, they decided to become the world's most terrifying saints. They would stop at nothing; they would storm the very gates of heaven. For as Patrick told them, quoting the words of Jesus in Saint Luke's Gospel, "The kingdom of heaven suffereth violence, and the violent bear it away!"

The Irish believed Patrick; they believed what he told them about God, about themselves, and about the goodness of creation. They believed him because of his courage: he was not afraid of them—even though he knew that during his many years in Ireland his life was in constant danger. As he tells us, "Every day I am ready to be murdered, betrayed, enslaved—whatever may come my way. But I am not afraid of any of these things, because of the promises of heaven; for I have put myself in the hands of God Almighty."

The Irish believed Patrick when he spoke of the boundless love of God because Patrick was himself so loving. He dedicated his life to them with a generosity beyond human understanding.

But it was just this generosity that troubled the British bishops, that made them imagine that Patrick must be up to no good. They would certainly never have thought to preach to the barbarians, so they thought Patrick must be getting something out of this. Was he charging for baptism, they wondered? When he consecrated a new bishop, was he taking something under the table?

No one had ever preached to barbarians, because no one thought barbarians were human. Even though Jesus—five centuries before—had clearly instructed his disciples to "preach to all nations," they simply had not done it. But Patrick trusted in God and believed the promises of God—that the Irish, too, could belong to that "great multitude, which no one could count, from every nation, race, people, and tongue," that the Irish, too, were God's People. So by returning to Ireland with the gospel, Patrick was doing something revolutionary. And revolutionaries are always misunderstood, especially by crabbed, smug, self-satisfied, comfortable, craven, ungenerous souls—like the British bishops.

The British bishops and the continental bishops and the African bishops were always talking about sinfulness and evil. They were vividly aware of human limitations. They were particularly down on the female half of humanity, whom they were fond of comparing to cesspools. Patrick left all this gloom and doom and anti-woman meanness behind him. The Fathers of the church looked into the hearts of human beings and saw human sinfulness—the dark side. Patrick looked into human hearts and saw the bright side—that even warriors and murderers could become peacemakers, even slave traders could become liberators, even barbarians could take their place among the nobility of heaven. He brought the Irish the gospel of salvation, but he left behind the hand wringing and tsk-tsking, so that early Irish Christianity had such bounce and playfulness to it that it became the happiest and most celebratory form of Christianity ever known. And it was such a welcoming kind of Christianity! It welcomed both women and men to high church office; its clergy did not set themselves apart but joined with lay people as equal partners, equal children of God. It took special care of the poor and the sick; and the Irish, knowing how marginalized they had once been, were always on the lookout to welcome those whom others rejected. In Ireland, no one turned away a stranger from the door; everyone, however tattered, had to be received with high style and princely generosity, for, as they said to one another, "often, often, often comes the Christ in the stranger's guise."

Patrick and his joyful Christians are calling out to us now across the centuries. They call out to the people of the United States of America, which has recently enacted cruel legislation that will make the hungry hungrier and the poor poorer. The richest nation in the world already has more poor children than any other Western democracy. With this new legislation that number is about to double. But these ancient men and women of Ireland are telling each of us that we must find a way, that we cannot let the flame of hope be extinguished in the lives of poor Americans and that we cannot turn our backs on the stranger in our midst. For "often, often, often comes the Christ in the stranger's guise."

These ancient Irish Christians call out to the Irish-American organizers of the St. Patrick's Day parades in Boston and New York, asking why they must exclude certain sons and daughters of Patrick from their festivities. Indeed, Patrick and his Christians are calling out to all of us. The Christianity that Patrick planted in Ireland is a model for us here and now, a model of tenderness and fellow human feeling, a model of generosity and courage, a model of the beautiful belief that we are surrounded by providence, that God's creation is good and full of hope and healing, and that "he who died for us" is speaking to each one of us in our hearts, if only we will stop and listen.

The great religious figure in Ireland after Patrick was his convert Brigid, she whom he described as "a blessed woman, Irish by birth, noble, extraordinarily beautiful— a true adult—whom I baptized." She became high abbess of Kildare, a woman to whom bishops reported.

Here is her grace before meals, a fitting grace before any evening meal, and an abiding reminder of Irish compassion and openheartedness:

I should like a great lake of finest ale
For the King of kings.
I should like a table of the choicest food
For the family of heaven.
Let the ale be made from the fruits of faith,
And the food be forgiving love.

I should welcome the poor to my feast,
For they are God's children.
I should welcome the sick to my feast,
For they are God's joy.
Let the poor sit with Jesus at the highest place,
And the sick dance with the angels.

God bless the poor,
God bless the sick,
And bless our human race.
God bless our food,
God bless our drink,
All homes, O God, embrace.

May God embrace your home and my home, and may we all, in the spirit of Patrick and Brigid, open our arms wide to embrace all the children of God.

Author Biography

Thomas Cahill is the author of *How the Irish Saved Civilization* and *The Gifts of the Jews.*

I first met Madeleine L'Engle through her writing. Interested in the new physics, I picked up her *A Wrinkle in Time* to see how she had turned such abstractions into a story. Next I read her novel *The Love Letters*. When I met her twenty years later, she was a character stepping out of her own fiction. I was almost surprised to find she had quite a physical self.

Virginia Stem Owens

4
Looking for Truth in the Age of Information

Virginia Stem Owens

Thomas S. Kuhn invented the term *paradigm shift* for his book *The Structure of Scientific Revolutions,* to designate the way the human activity we call science progresses not by the slow accretion of knowledge, the way barnacles grow on the bottom of a boat, but by sudden jolts and bursts of creativity. He allows that much of science is done slowly and methodically with the scientist acting as rational problem-solver who devises hypotheses, then tests them through experimentation. But this, he says, is only the mopping-up operation after some truly new theory, like a revolutionist's grenade, has exploded old ways of thinking.

Children, however, have the advantage of operating by still-malleable models for the world. Their paradigms can be shaped, rather than undergoing the more cumbersome process of shifting. They are still open to any number of possibilities for putting together reality's big picture. Madeleine L'Engle, in her time-travel books, pressed a dexterous thumb into the wet clay of her young readers' minds and transformed their universe almost effortlessly.

Most scientific revolutions are fomented among adults, however. As such, they are generally as rebellious, seditious, and contumacious as any political insurrection, though fortunately not usually so bloody. These mutinies against the old guard turn the scientific world upside down, setting it on its ear. Their instigators are seen, at least initially, as traitors and renegades. Which indeed they are. They insist on throwing out all the hard-won positions of the preceding generation and starting over again from the ground up.

And they suffer the usual fate of rebels. Their thesis proposals are rejected or they cannot find an institute to fund their research or a scholarly journal willing to publish their work. (Even though literature supposedly thrives on innovation, L'Engle's *A Wrinkle in Time* had trouble finding a publisher as well, since it did not fit the mold for "children's" fiction.) Scientific innovators actually have to work in isolation and keep their projects secret for fear of becoming professional pariahs.

But later—sometimes after their death—when the scientific community has accepted their discovery, a shock wave begins to rumble through the general culture, resulting in a paradigm shift. A lone scientist, working in isolation and against adversity, dislodges a stone on the mountainside, and soon the whole slope gives way, crushing beneath it our preconceived notions—the pictures we carry in our heads of how the world works. These pictures are so fundamental to our understanding, our *shared* understanding, that their disruption affects all areas of our lives, not just our academic interests in botany or geology.

Galileo's revolutionary move from an earth-centered universe to a sun-centered one is always used as the prime example of paradigm shift. But the human race already had dealt with a number before Galileo's. Heraclitus, the holistic Greek, had seen reality as a flowing river of irrecoverable time. Later, Democritus revised this picture, breaking reality into tiny bits of falling matter he named atoms. And, after Galileo, Newton made the world into a machine for us, its gears grinding away in steady and predictable regularity.

Each of these pictures, or paradigms, had repercussions. The shock wave of each scientific revolution spreads outward to rock the boat of the entire culture. Darwin, for example, writing innocently enough about the fauna of a faraway island off the coast of Ecuador, nearly swamped the ship of Western civilization, whose inhabitants were still shivering from the drenching Newton's clockwork cosmos had given them. Things had only about a half-century to settle down after Darwin before we were hit with Einstein's theory of relativity. Each of these paradigm shifts has required a radical restructuring of the picture we carry around in our heads of what we call "the world" or "reality." And the process is not yet finished.

A major problem for us had been entropy, a piece of the puzzle left over from Newton's universe. Even Einstein and quantum mechanics had left the problem of entropy unresolved.

In Newton's universe, cause and effect ruled with an iron rod. You could never end up with more or less of either energy or matter than you started with, and you could count on that. That was the good news. The bad news was entropy—otherwise known as the Second Law of Thermodynamics. Briefly, all organized systems, whether stars or protozoa, tend inevitably toward a state of disorganization and death. Stars burn out; protozoa die and decay into so much biomass. Your coffee *always* cools off in the cup. It *never* gets hotter just sitting there. Batteries run down. Eventually, even gravity and the so-called "strong force" binding atomic nuclei together will dissipate. All that will be left of the universe then is a uniform, homogeneous goo.

This sad part of the story cast a shadow over the

imagination of the Western world. Entropy took on metaphysical connotations even for the most resolute logical positivist whose only response to this bleak cosmic future was a stiff upper lip. It colored William Faulkner's celebrated Nobel Prize speech where he pictures "the last ding-dong of doom" clanging and fading "from the last worthless rock hanging tideless in the last red and dying evening." Entropy is what sends Holden Caulfield into an adolescent spiritual tailspin in *Catcher in the Rye*. The optimism that had powered Western civilization since the Renaissance leaked away. How could human beings find the heart to go on in a universe where protein chains randomly coupled—according to Darwin—but simultaneously dissolved—according to Newton? Either way, we were lost in the cosmos, abandoned, of no ultimate worth, with no future.

No wonder every facet of the culture began to reflect this despair. The paradigm, the picture of reality we all shared, was pretty bleak. Intellectually and imaginatively, we were left to the mercy of those twin specters—chance and dissolution. The dominant religious establishment, the church, which had been in the business of paradigm building during its first millennium, was left to cool its heels at the door of the new temples—laboratories, observatories, and cyclotrons. Having renounced natural theology during the Reformation, it now had only an old manuscript in a confusing number of fragments from which to stitch together a picture of the world. And except for a couple of fanciful stories about how the world came to be, stories that focused on a single planet, the manuscript seemed to have little relevant information to offer.

In order to circumvent complete cultural schizophrenia, theologians came up with the two-truths theory. Science, they said, deals with physical truth and the Bible deals with spiritual truth. Do not expect laboratories to tell you anything about God, and do not expect the

Bible to tell you anything about the material world. The Bible was not intended as a scientific textbook, we were told. One of the propounders of the Big Bang Theory, Robert Wilson, when questioned about the biblical version of creation in a television interview, observed that the Bible is about love, not science. A far cry from Dante, who had claimed it was love that drove the stars.

I do not want to disparage the cultural tension in which we have all lived for decades now. Sincerely pious people of intellectual integrity have responded to the problem as Robert Wilson did. The two-truths theory may well have been the best answer we could come up with at the time, short of completely withdrawing from the culture into an intellectual ghetto—which has, at certain times in history, been itself an honorable option. But certain new questions are being asked by scientists now that may help heal this bifurcation of reality into a physical world and a spiritual one. Our picture of reality, splintered into fragments during the last paradigm shift, may be on the verge of having its timepieces click into place again.

About the time the Atomic Age blew itself up at Hiroshima, the Information Age was being born, appropriately enough at the Bell Telephone Laboratories with a shy mathematician named Claude Shannon serving as midwife.[1] He was beginning to see that limiting the component parts of physical reality to matter and energy alone left too many holes in the picture. Matter and energy, left to their own devices, are not enough to explain the world as we experience it. Shannon started, as all revolutionaries do, with basic questions the human race has always pondered. How come there is something instead of nothing? Especially since, statistically, the most probable state of the cosmos is chaos. How did any shape ever emerge out of sheer disorganized energy? How did something as structured as atoms get clumped together instead of continuing to drift ineffectually apart?

Why did atoms hook up into molecules and molecules into complex proteins? And once there were living organisms, why did they tend to get ever more complicated?

Shannon's work actually amounted to a referendum on the Second Law of Thermodynamics. From the far side of a scientific revolution, the questions always appear self-evident. But up till then, no one had thought to ask how you could have both evolution (whether on an atomic, chemical, or biological level) and entropy at the same time. Evolution and entropy appear to be contradictory conditions. Either things get more organized, more structured, or they tend inevitably toward disorganization and dissolution. How could you have it both ways? Yet our experience of the world seemed to show that is the way it is.

Shannon's answer was ultimately labeled Information Theory. In exploring these questions, he investigated how a message can survive in the midst of haphazard disorder or "noise." How, for example, can your ear distinguish the sound of a conversation from the other noises assaulting it at the same moment and then integrate these filtered sounds into a meaningful message? How can your eye distinguish the print you are reading now from the paper and decode the message? Or your friend's face from the visual background, so that you can recognize the same person in another setting?

The answer, Shannon discovered, was in a critical balance achieved between two factors—redundancy and uncertainty. On the one hand, you have to know what to expect and have a certain amount of expectation satisfied. On the other hand, there has to be a certain degree of surprise.

The structure of language, for example, is redundant and repetitive. We expect words to come in certain sequences rather than at random. In English, that means the verb usually follows the subject. Our words are not made up of a random distribution of twenty-six letters.

Instead, they appear in predictable clusters. If all the *e*s were left blank on this page, you would still be able to figure out the message, simply because in English we can predict more *e*s than *q*s or *z*s or any other letter. On the sentence level, our system of grammar prepares us to expect a noun to follow a preposition. It gives us a limited set of expectations which are ordinarily met. The reliable repetition of a pattern is an information system's protection against error.

Redundancy is indeed what makes complexity possible. The more complex a system, whether in a machine or a living organism, the more likely one of its parts is to fail. (If you have a car with computerized fuel injection, power windows and locks, and electric seats, you know what I mean.) Back-up programs (another term for redundancy) keep complex systems running in the face of malfunctions. And to insure accuracy in a transmitted message, one must have a copy to check it against—another form of redundancy. Developmental instructions are coded, for instance, in every cell in your body, not simply stored in one central location.

But just as redundancy is necessary to information, so is uncertainty. If you were able to predict completely what I was going to say next, there would be no point in my saying it. The very certainty would make the message useless.

The human mind must have a definite degree of order to work with. It cannot deal with pure chaos. Presented with random figures, say cloud formations or inkblots, it sets about immediately to *shape* them, imagining that they look like elephants or butterflies. But the brain must also have a degree of looseness to work with, some uncertainty, some unexpectedness, or it shuts down altogether. Too much redundancy, too much predictability—like a dripping faucet—becomes unbearable.

Still, messages encoded over fiber optic cables by human beings are one thing, but messages built into the structure of the universe itself? Shannon's discovery of Information Theory was enough to shake our lost-in-the-cosmos paradigm to its foundations. It proved to be applicable to "natural" structures as well as manmade systems. It was essential, for instance, to unraveling the puzzling double-helix structure of DNA by Watson and Crick, who discovered that such a design provided chromosomes with both the necessary information to reproduce themselves and also the very code for deciphering that information.

Suddenly, the specter of randomness that haunted our cultural imagination began to dissipate. Perhaps we were not, after all, awash in a witless universe of meaningless "noise." In fact, in just about every discipline now, some town crier is running through the streets announcing, "Rejoice! There is order in the universe after all!" In economics, demography, physics, biology, thermodynamics—in all areas of scientific investigation—order is the new watchword. Late-twentieth-century science has rediscovered a plan, a pattern in the cosmos. There is a voice embedded in the very heart of matter.

The application of Information Theory to biology has especially put heart into the human enterprise once more. For one thing, it has pushed back the rigid confines of a dreary Darwinism and random selection. But even more importantly, it has given us a picture of reality in which information is not just a manmade product. Information has become a full member of a reality triumvirate made up of matter, energy, *and* information. All three of these exist apart from us, even prior to us. Therefore, information, message, meaning are not simply concepts we invented, but, like the rest of the physical world, were here before we arrived on the scene.

I am not sure the full implications of such a paradigm have yet dawned on many even in the scientific community. If there is indeed information buried in the heart of matter itself, giving it commands, instructing it how to behave, where is this message coming from? What is its source? Surely information presumes an informer, and a message, an author. Otherwise, scientists had better get busy devising a new vocabulary to describe what they mean.

So far, I have discovered that most scientists and writers deal with this problem in one of two ways. The first is a holdover from the eighteenth-century Enlightenment—the old familiar Nature with a capital *N*. When God began to disappear from the intellectual scene in the eighteenth century, we still needed some way of talking about a motive force behind physical phenomena. A personified Nature stepped in to fill that niche. Nature became some vaguely mythologized figure to which one could attach verbs of intention without bothering too much about theological content. As in "Nature abhors a vacuum." Or "natural selection." And today, otherwise perfectly sensible scientists and writers sustain this myth by speaking without a blush about, for instance, "nature at her most inventive."

Consider, for example, the sentence taken from a book on Information Theory published in 1982: "The principle of information specifies the forms which matter takes, so that things are literally 'informed' by an idea and strive to fulfill it." A thrilling concept, and one not unfamiliar to anyone who has read Psalm 19. That sentence, however, is followed by this one: "Nature builds according to the data which instructs matter to change in a particular way." Is the author using *Nature* only to fill a grammatical gap? Are we not supposed to take the subject of his sentence seriously? Or is he indeed a believer in a kind of vague vitalism? I doubt that he has considered the question seriously. But I also believe that he represents the general cultural acceptance of a mythological Nature.

Another more carefully thought out answer to the question of who is doing the directing, or what is the source of this information buried in physical reality, comes from scientists such as Ilya Prigogine, the Nobel Laureate in chemistry specializing in thermodynamic systems, who brooks no sentimental twaddle about Nature and her inventions. Instead, he uses the term *self-organizing systems,* a description growing in popularity among scientific disciplines. He applies the term to certain occasions when a seemingly disordered system, containing little pattern or information, unexpectedly develops a structure. This happens in systems as diverse as pots of boiling water, genetic mutations, and political parties. Prigogine believes there is a hitherto unrecognized principle that pushes these systems toward states of greater complexity—the opposite of entropy. He says,

> This is something completely new, something that yields a new scientific intuition about the nature of our universe. It is totally against the classical thermodynamic view that information must always degrade. It is, if you will, something profoundly optimistic.

He points out that in certain chemical reactions, molecules respond not simply to local circumstances, bouncing off one another or hooking up their stray electrons in ways predicted by the laws of classical physics, but that they can actually adjust their behavior to the larger parent organism with which they are not in direct contact. This ability, as he says, shows the organism to be "vastly different than the mere sum of its parts."[2]

As Prigogine said, this is a profoundly optimistic scientific discovery. It breaks through the rigidity of the paradigm we have learned to call *determinism.* But so far, Prigogine's way of explaining such astonishing behavior is to call such occurrences *self-organizing systems,* a description that begs the question on only a slightly more sophisticated level than attributing it to an intentional, mythological Nature. For what is the origin of this mysterious "self" that has the power to organize matter and imbue it with knowledge? Does not a "self" imply intention, will, desire—qualities we do not ordinarily attribute to a pot of boiling water?

These kinds of questions send us back to the Bible. For we, of all creatures the most self-conscious, are not conscious of having organized ourselves into being. Indeed, it seems much more likely that the message imbedded in the matter from which we were formed came from a Self infinitely more capable and knowledgeable than ourselves. Where was I when my body was being "knit together in my mother's womb," or even before that—when I was "intricately woven in the depths of the earth"? It seems a saner guess that some other, some infinitely more able, Self "beheld my unformed substance" and gave it the necessary information to become me.[3]

Even the prologue to John's Gospel takes on a new dimension when read not simply as ornamental poeticizing but as a reliable description of unified reality—not a reality split into spiritual and physical realms. "In the beginning was the Word, and the Word was with God, and the Word was God. He was in the beginning with God. All things came into being through him, and without him not one thing came into being."[4] *This*, the Bible says, is how there came to be something instead of nothing. This is the kind of self necessary for organizing creation. This Word is the indissoluble and essential link between spirit and matter.

Nor is its message imbedded in human beings only. The Bible instructs us on that score also, in all those passages, dismissed for centuries now as merely metaphorical, pretty trimming on the psalms, about "knowledge" possessed by a supposedly inanimate universe. In the Bible, trees and rocks are said to have knowledge. God speaks to the earth and it obeys; "whether for correction, or for his land, or for love, he causes it to happen" (Job 39). "Day to day pours forth speech, and night to night declares knowledge" (Psalm 19). All these passages are proving to be not, after all, mere holdovers from animism. Or perhaps more accurately, animism retains a shred of our discarded intuitive recognition of this knowledge in the heart of matter.

The physical world, scientists are learning, responds to messages from someone. I suspect Madeleine L'Engle has a pretty good idea of who that is. The picture of reality she presents is not a clockwork mechanism but a living universe, guided by an intelligence, an intention, a self. Some people, accustomed to living either in a machine or in a world of watertight compartments for the physical and the spiritual, will be frightened to wake up in this kind of world. But Madeleine L'Engle's fortunate readers, already introduced to the infinite possibilities of reality, will no doubt be delighted to have their world turned upside down.

Author Biography

Virginia Stem Owens has written more than a dozen books on a wide range of topics from metaphysics to media, including a series of mysteries set in her native Texas. She has lectured on physics and Information Theory and their connection to aesthetics at a number of colleges.

She is on the editorial board of *Books & Culture*. She also serves as director of the Milton Center, an institute in Wichita, Kansas, which supports excellence in Christian letters and which helped form the Chrysostom Society, of which Madeleine L'Engle is a charter member.

My wife and I first knew Madeleine L'Engle from reading her children's books to our children. We delighted in this: the stories were so true, the reality of God and the complexities of evil so honestly and accurately written. She became a staunch ally in childrearing and gospel witness. Later we found that her adult fiction and meditative writings were as good for us as the earlier books had been for our children. Now, in the community of friends known as the Chrysostom Society, we enjoy in her person the taste for truth and the appetite for righteousness that we have so long enjoyed in her books.

Eugene H. Peterson

5
Gospel Quartet: Jesus in Four Voices

Eugene H. Peterson

Storytellers are our most honored users of language. In every civilization and culture, the storyteller holds the center. Story is the purest and most democratic use of the language: young mothers murmuring lullabies to their infants, country singers spinning ballads, young people telling ghost stories around a campfire, and preachers telling the "old, old story" from a grand pulpit, poets and novelists and playwrights published and unpublished. Madeleine L'Engle's magnificent storytelling is conspicuous in this company; for close to fifty years her stories have nurtured a Christian shape to the way we understand and live our lives.

Our premier storytellers are Matthew, Mark, Luke, and John. More, and better, than any others they create the space and work out the plot in which we find the place and meaning of our lives. They do it by telling The Jesus Story, which reveals the two things that we most need to know, *God* and *ourselves*. God: Jesus reveals the character and action of the one who brought us into being out of nothing and has designs upon us for all eternity.

And ourselves: Jesus reveals the way in which we can enter into this beingness and eternity as fully alive participants and not as amused or disgruntled or envious spectators sitting on a curbstone watching life parade away from us down the street.

Matthew, Mark, Luke, and John were the first persons to write down this Jesus story of God and ourselves. They all tell the same story, but each in his own distinctive way—writers are makers after all, not copiers. In the last couple of centuries there have been many well-intentioned attempts to reduce these highly personal and distinctive writers to impersonal "sources." This has had the unfortunate effect of obscuring and sometimes destroying the very stories that our Gospel writers have set before us as gifts of the Holy Spirit.

Some scholars have supposed that by getting "behind" the stories, sleuthing for what they call "sources," they could serve us forth a better or truer "truth." But most writers are highly offended when people get more interested in the contents of their wastebaskets and filing cabinets than in the books they write: "Read the story! The meaning is in the story, not in the information in the story. Read the story the way I wrote it!"

Our ancestors, the early followers of Jesus, gave precisely such attention to our four writers. They not only recognized their fourfold authority that provided a reliable account of God's revelation in Jesus, but gave each of them the dignity of writers with a story to tell and a particular and irreplaceable way of telling it. They did not pick their favorites and campaign for a "winner." The community's consensus was that we need all four writers, each in his own voice, and yet all there together if we are going to get the story complete. If Matthew, Mark, Luke, and John were singers we might call them a Gospel Quartet: Jesus in Four Voices.

Storytellers are our primary truth-tellers; they always

have been and they always will be. The act of storytelling is embedded inextricably in the act of speech. Not long after we are capable of connecting one word with another we demand stories; and not long after that we begin telling them. Storytelling is essential to the cultivation and maintenance of our human identity. It is also essential to our Christian identity—and for the same reasons. We image-of-God humans have a story shape. Narrative constitutes the verbal structure that shows us who we are, where we come from, and where we are going. It primes the pump of our participation in "story-reality," that is, life with plot and action and character as over against ideas and numbers, abstractions and lessons. Story is not something "made up" about us—something exterior, something tacked on to our biology or history: story *reveals* and *invites*.

But prior to being a human act, the form of language most common and congenial to the human condition, storytelling is a theological act, which is to say, a God act. *God* tells stories. In the opening pages of Holy Scripture, Genesis, we find God using words to make the world and then, at a somewhat later time, using words to tell us the story of the making. In the Gospel rewriting of Genesis by St. John, we find the same thing: The Word (Jesus) by which everything comes into being using words (Jesus again) to tell us the meaning of what is. Creation (Genesis) and Salvation (John) are set alongside each other as, precisely, *stories:* language used to make what was not there previously (creation *ex nihilo),* and, at the same time, reveal the meaning of its making. When the making and the meaning occur on the same page, we have a story. Language used in the form of Story is our most common and most accessible access to the reality that we enter so abruptly from the womb and then so gradually find our place in through our long growing up and growing old. Language, it turns out, is a basic essential in the spirituality of the human species. The *way* we use language, not just our capacity for it. Language is spirit into word.

When we use language to tell stories, we are working close to the bone of language, using words to simultaneously *make* and *reveal*. And not just a fragment or shard of something or other, but a coherent *world*— plot, character, place, purpose, names and numbers, wisdom and insight, origin and relationships and purpose. This is what words are for; this is the way words were used by God from the beginning (Genesis and John) and are intended to be used by us humans: both to make and to reveal the making.

The reason that we need a continuous train of storytellers is that sin disrupts, and sometimes destroys, the thread of narrative that is our lives, leaving us story-less, plot-less. In that condition we are vulnerable to predators who are determined to exploit our lives for functions and goals that feed their ambition. If they find us in a depersonalized state, we can be used in impersonal ways. If they come upon us in a plotless condition, they can fit us into slots in their daytimers and production schedules. But if we are adequately "storied," they have a harder time with us.

Four master storytellers wrote the books that tell the story of Jesus. The story they told and the way they told it provide the text that the followers of Jesus have read ever since to get in on the making/revealing words of this "word made flesh." For Christians, the four books are foundational for understanding and responding to the two sets of documents ("testaments") that make up their Bibles, the Holy Scriptures that continue to make and reveal God's work. Nothing comparable has ever been written.

Matthew, Mark, Luke, and John: Storytellers. It is not often enough noticed that they were, each of them, supreme storytellers. The task of writing the primary documents for the Christian community was assigned to storytellers. We more often designate them *evangelists*. And that designation is surely accurate, for they were preachers of "good news"—that God is present in Jesus to inaugurate the kingdom of God and save us from our sins. But the *way* they wrote what they preached was in story.

Jesus is the origin and originator of the story. St. Paul was the first to write it in a sentence: "[Jesus is] . . . the first-born of all creation. . . . He is before all things, and in him all things hold together" (Colossians 1:15, 17). Each of our four writers takes that concise, skeletal dogma and elaborates it into a full-bodied flesh-and-blood story. In collecting and arranging the documents that make up our New Testament, the Christian community decided to set these four stories rather than Paul's precise dogma first. *This* is the way to begin—with story, not dogma. There is no getting behind this beginning. There is no getting around this beginning. To begin life, the understanding of life, the salvation of life gone to the dogs, the healing of life crippled and diseased, the sanctifying of life trivialized and cursed is to begin with the stories *of* Jesus, not statements *about* Jesus.

Not many in the Christian community contest the primacy of Jesus. But surprisingly there are a great many who contest (or simply ignore) the canonical primacy of *story*. Inspirational slogans, apologetic arguments, grammatical analyses, historical reconstructions, consumer psychologies, meaningful encounters, bullying threats, and energizing challenges crowd out the story. The name *Jesus* occurs often enough in these various and sundry verbal projects, but the story is more often than not ignored or overlooked. It is alarming, and also dismaying, how frequently people in our time utilize the Jesus story as a word-warehouse from which they take items that serve their verbal designs but ignore the story itself.

Story is not, of course, the only way to speak of Jesus, or even in every circumstance the most appropriate way. Many forms of speech are necessarily employed in presenting and explaining, in persuading and guiding men and women in response to Jesus. But it is significant that St. Paul, our first theologian, most of whose letters were written before the Gospels, is only allowed to appear on the pages of the Scripture canon after the four Gospel writers have had ample and leisurely opportunity to give us the story. When the story is first, other forms of speech maintain accuracy and force; if the story is secondary (or relegated to the sidelines entirely, as it is so often), Jesus is too easily distilled from a particular and complex person embodying all the purposes of God in personal relationships with all sorts and conditions of men and women into an abstract principle or a general truth or a timeless ideal. There is no way in which we can even begin to account for the intricacy and detail, dynamic and relational ups and down, swerves and tangents involved in our lives, let alone the life of Jesus, without telling a story.

I am interested in recovering an appreciation of our four Gospel writers as storytellers—these one-of-a-kind writers who used words to make and reveal life, the life of Christ, and the life of Christ in us. I want to assist, insofar as I am able, in the recovery of the indispensable personal use of words, the trinitarian complexity of language for a people who are bombarded daily, hourly, with weapons-words, seductive words, depersonalizing words. And in the process recover, in the vast cosmos of the gospel, our lives made large and revealed as saved by God's word.

Matthew, Mark, Luke, and John were modest writers (not a typical trait among writers), and none claim authorship. But the early generations of those who read them wrote in the writers' names soon enough. They not only named the writers, but kept the four together as a company: Matthew, Mark, Luke, and John. The four Gospel writers have kept congenial company ever since. An old nursery rhyme addresses them in prayer,

Matthew, Mark, Luke, and John
Bless the bed I lie upon.
And if I should die before I wake,
I pray the Lord my soul to take.

They appear again in the more sophisticated context of Robert Lowell's poem "At the Indian Killer's Grave":

John, Matthew, Luke and Mark,
Gospel me to the Garden . . .[1]

Lowell's use of *gospel* as a transitive verb catches the conviction of Christian readers that these four stories take us someplace, someplace that we want to go. They are not entertainment or speculation—they are vehicles.

St. Matthew

St. Matthew is the first of the four Gospel storytellers. He may not have been the first to take pen in hand to write his story, but he comes first in the order of our reading the stories. This lead-off position is utilized to create something entirely new, the Old Testament.

Prior to Matthew there was no Old Testament. There was simply the Bible (the Mikra, the Tenak), the thirty-nine documents that composed the holy scriptures of the people of Israel. But in the act of writing his Gospel, Matthew re-imagined these scriptures as a "testament" to Jesus Christ. And it worked. His imagination caught the imagination of the followers of Jesus. Thanks to Matthew, this Hebrew Bible was changed into a Christian Bible. This is, on the face of it, an incredible accomplishment. It was done without argument or committee, without council or edict. He simply wrote his story of Jesus in such a way that these Hebrew writings, the holy scriptures of Judaism, changed under the eyes of those who read them into a Christian document, Christian scripture.

In order to appreciate both what Matthew did and how he did it we must note what a formidable task he accomplished. The *Law and the Prophets*, to use the usual first-century designation, has enormous authority. As a devout Jew, Matthew could not ignore the Hebrew scriptures. Nor could he repudiate them. But how could he avoid being swamped by these weighty books? How could he write anything that would be anything more than a footnote to the majesty of these writings?

We see it take place before our eyes: Matthew converts the Hebrew Bible into Christian scripture by treating it with immense respect. He refers to it constantly in such a way that without changing a word, it is re-fashioned before our eyes. Sometimes we say that Matthew uses the OT to prove Jesus, or authenticate Jesus. It works the other way around: Jesus proves the OT; Jesus authenticates the OT. Skillful Matthew does this quietly, without raising his voice, hardly calling attention to what he is doing. By the time he has finished his story of Jesus, he has "transformed the Bible of his day into the Old Testament. The Bible of Israel became the Old Testament in the process of his writing."[2]

Matthew begins his story deeply rooted in the Jewish world. By his last chapter he has carried us far beyond the Jewish world. From chapter 1 to chapter 28 we move from the local to the universal, from forty-two named Jewish men and women to all of humankind. In writing his book Matthew has changed from Jew to Christian.

In the course of telling his story, Matthew writes "that

the word might be fulfilled which was spoken by the Lord through the prophet." Thirteen times, he sets down the phrase. Forty-eight times he quotes from the Hebrew scriptures; allusions to Law and Prophets are pervasive—there is not a page of his text in which they do not occur. Matthew makes sure that we realize that there is hardly a detail in Jesus' life, and practically none in his death, that was not anticipated, prepared for, and written in the holy books of the Hebrew people.

Matthew is writing the story of Jesus the Christ—an absolutely new thing, a unique revelation—God in human flesh, incarnation. But he conveys the uniqueness not by distancing the story from the past but by acknowledging it, giving it its due, paying proper respects to all his storytelling ancestors.

There is nothing quite so suspect in matters of spirituality as the claim to originality. If an idea or practice is presented as a novelty—the "latest" or "unprecedented" or "original"—it is almost surely wrong.

It is possible, even probable, that without Matthew, Christians would have had no Old Testament; this great body of revelation would have eventually been lost to the Christian church. The Law and the Prophets of the Hebrew people would have entered the library shelves along with the Koran of the Muslims and the Vedas of the Hindus. There was a strong movement in the early Christian centuries to get rid of these Hebrew scriptures and make a clean start (Marcion). And there are plenty of people today who boycott them, wanting to save themselves the trouble (they think) of including their past into their life of salvation. But all mature, healthy, sound spirituality has past and precedent. If we choose to ignore it, we end up repeating all the old mistakes ourselves; or, what is worse, removing huge chunks of our lives from the fulfilling and sanctifying power of the Spirit of Jesus Christ.

Matthew roots his story deep in the soil of Jewishness.

He saturates his narrative with affirmations of Jewish/Hebrew precedence and continuity. Is this wise? Is this not far too narrow a base on which to construct a story that is intended to reach everyone and at all times and everywhere?

We might think so. But look at the ending. The last words of Jesus as Matthew gives them are this: "All authority has been given to me. Therefore go and make disciples of all nations, baptizing them in the name of the Father and of the Son and of the Holy Spirit, and teaching them to obey everything I have commanded you. And surely I will be with you always, to the very end of the age" (28:18-20). Matthew has reversed the meaning of the Bible (OT) by experiencing it no longer as the last word for the Jews but as the preparatory word for everyone. In Matthew's last sentence the "world suddenly grows to gigantic proportions."[3]

St. Mark

Our earliest traditions tell us that Mark wrote his Gospel in Rome in the company and presumably under the direction of St. Peter. Peter, leader of the original twelve apostles, placed first in all the listings of the apostles, is in Rome being readied for martyrdom. In his presence and under his influence Mark wrote his story of Jesus.

Somewhere along the way St. Mark acquired a nickname: *Colobodactylus*, "stumpfingered." One suggestion accounting for the name is that Mark was a large man whose fingers were disproportionately small—stubby fingers. It sounds like an affectionate nickname, the kind we give to friends that we kid around with: Shorty, Slim, Blue-eyes, Kitten. Colobodactylus, "Stumpfingers." It is easy to imagine that it originated in the circle of friends in Rome who saw him working away day by day writing his Gospel, watching those short, thick fingers push that pen (stylus) back and forth across the parchment, jokingly noting the incongruity between the clumsy-looking fingers holding the pen and the swift-paced drama of the sentences as they were laid down. There may have been at the same time a joking hint of congruity between Mark's conspicuously inelegant hands and what Reynolds Price calls the "pawky roughness of language."[4]

The apostle whom he served also had a nickname: *Peter*, or *Rock*. But unlike his master's, Mark's nickname did not stick—only in Rome was Mark known as Colobodactylus. Tradition has it that after Peter's martyrdom, Mark went to Alexandria where he became the bishop. *Stumpfinger* probably did not seem appropriate for a bishop, and so he recovered his proper name.

The Mark story-telling is fast-paced, austere, and compellingly dramatic. Mark does not linger, does not elaborate, does not explain, does not digress. Event follows event, narrative details piling up pell-mell, seemingly without design. The design is there all right, but unobtrusive and hidden. Mark as storyteller is entirely unpretentious. He hides his art, stripping the story of all finery or sophistication in either diction or syntax. This is drama without melodrama. Every detail is chosen with meticulous care and is put in its place with great skill. The carefully rationed accumulation of narrative lines moves Jesus from the obscurity of itinerant teaching and healing in out-of-the-way Galilee into a suddenly flood-lighted public notice in Jerusalem. There Roman and Jew, fearing that he will prove fatal to their respective political and religious regimes, kill him. And here is the marvel: without the narrator's intruding into the story with comment or announcement, we end up convinced that Jesus is the anointed of God, here to save us from our sins and show us the way to live rightly: follow this person!

This most unpretentious of storytellers (Stumpfingers!) has written the most demanding and revealing of stories.

But alongside this there is another feature that requires notice. Though Mark writes his story under the influence of the greatest of the apostles, Peter, he practically writes him out of the story. The true relation between Jesus and his followers was at stake here. Peter as the lead apostle has the potential for moving into a place of prominence alongside Jesus. Mark makes sure that will not happen by portraying Peter as the lead sinner. If Peter as leader can be prevented from moving into the limelight with Jesus, it is accomplished for all Christians forever. And that is what Mark does. It may be his finest accomplishment as storywriter—in Peter's presence and under Peter's authority and influence, he keeps Peter from taking over the story. The glorification of Peter is blocked at the source. Whatever stellar qualities Peter acquired in his leadership and preaching in the early church are excised from the story and replaced by his weaknesses and failures. The Jesus story includes a colorful company of others, but none of them is presented in such a way as to obscure or compromise the unique and unprecedented centrality of Jesus. Peter is portrayed as a bungler, as a blasphemer, and as a faithless human being. But not *merely* Peter, Peter as *leader*. For neither do the other chosen disciples become examples to look up to or follow. Thick-skulled and dull-witted, they turn out to be a pack of cowards. Hoskyns and Davey remark on the "staggering brutality" with which Mark writes the disciples out of any part of Jesus' work.[5]

Mark, in other words, tells this foundational Christian story in such a way as to prevent us from setting apart any of our leaders as spiritually upper-class, putting them on pedestals. This is a salvation story and the savior is Jesus. Nothing in the storytelling is permitted to divert our attention from Jesus. There is nothing here that will play into our preference for dealing with famous celebrities instead of the despised Jesus. There is nothing glamorous or inspiring about even the best of the apostles: every one, down to the last man and woman, is saved by grace.

Maintaining that simplicity and focus—that the gospel is God's initiative and grace in Jesus—has proved to be one of the most difficult things to maintain in the Christian community. In the course of the generations, Mark's storytelling has not prevented us from developing celebrity cults, elevating Peter and others to prominence, and thereby providing seemingly easier ways of dealing with our souls than dealing with God in Jesus. And it has not prevented us from being diverted by spiritual and religious novelties that promise shortcuts to soul-entertainment. But Mark's story continues to provide the honest ground to which we all return from our God-detours and soul-diversions.

St. Luke

The distinctive mark in Luke's storytelling is that he wrote two stories of Jesus in parallel. The first is the story of Jesus in his own right; the second is the story of Jesus reproduced in the lives of his first generation of followers.

Because the two stories are separated by John's Gospel in our New Testaments, the unity of Luke's story is sometimes missed. But the two stories (the Gospel of Jesus Christ and the Acts of the Apostles) are obviously intended to be read as two parts of a single story: they are both addressed to "Theophilus"; they are of approximately the same length; and they are roughly symmetrical.

Luke begins the story of Jesus on a world stage shared by Jewish heritage (Zechariah and Elizabeth) and Roman rule (Caesar Augustus); the story of Jesus' followers ends on a world stage shared, again, by Jews (as they listen to Paul teach about Jesus, Acts 28:17-27) in the capital of the world empire, Rome ("all who came to see him . . . without hindrance. . . ." Acts 28:30-31). The Gospel, initiated by angel messages from heaven and Ceasar's decree from Rome, contracts geographically from Rome to Galilee, Samaria, Judea, and a final focus in Jerusalem; the Acts expands outwardly from Jerusalem through Judea, Galilee, Samaria, throughout the Mediterranean basin, and finally to a world platform in Rome.

The effect of the symmetrical stories is to convince readers that everything that Jesus did continues in the life of his followers. Detail after detail is seen in parallel: the teaching, the preaching, the people, the acceptance, the opposition, the religious and political court trials. But the Gospel begins widely and moves to a tightly coiled concentration of energy in Jerusalem; the Acts narrates the release and uncoiling of that energy from Jerusalem into all languages and lands. Jesus, the Christ, is conceived by the Holy Spirit in the Gospel story and begins the work of salvation; Jesus' followers, the Christians, are filled by the Holy Spirit in the Acts story and carry the same work of salvation into all the world.

Nothing is more common in the world of spirituality than the reification of the life of the soul into a book, spirituality thing-ified into something studied in a library or school, or honored as holy tradition. The further a story is removed from its originating historical context, the greater the possibility that it loses historicity—the immediate actuality of person and place, emotion and action. The aura of a hoary past begins to develop around the story and even though much admired, the sense that it is part and parcel of everyone's life, *my* life, becomes more and more remote. Luke's two volumes insist that the life of Jesus is reproducible in my life, your life. Nothing that I do or say is exempt from the formative words and actions of Jesus. Everything that Jesus lived is experienceable by men and women, young and old, whatever land in which we live, whatever language we speak. But whatever the land, language, and decade, it remains *Jesus'* life.

Luke makes extensive use of the life of Paul, whom he knew personally and well, to demonstrate that the life of Jesus is still the life of Jesus ("Christ who lives in me," Galatians 2:20) as it is lived by Christian disciples as they travel their various roads into "all the world."

With only a very few exceptions, most of us feel quite ordinary, with run-of-the-mill lives. When we encounter a truly extraordinary life, we are impressed, we admire, but we do not dream that it has much to do with us. We become spectators to such a life. And so one of the enduring tasks in relation to Jesus is to turn admiring spectators into participating disciples. This is what Luke does superbly. He says, in effect, that the story of Jesus does not end with Jesus; it continues in the lives of those who believe in him. The supernatural does not stop with Jesus. Luke makes it clear that these Christians he wrote about were no more spectators of Jesus than Jesus was a spectator of God—they are in on the action of God, God acting in them, God living in them.

There is an accompanying consequence: there are no longer any outsiders. The story of Jesus gathers everyone, quite literally *every one,* into its plot. Religion, left to itself, always becomes a club, an insiders' club from which the unqualified are barred. The instinct for belonging is deep within us; the easiest way to gratify that instinct is to create a manageable and congenial group of like-minded persons who have superior characteristics, and then exclude everyone else. Exclusion, of course, is far easier than inclusion—it requires virtually no effort at all, at least no *soul*-effort, neither intimacy nor love, neither generosity nor sacrifice, neither grace nor mercy. Being an "insider" is achieved simply by locking the door and taking precautions against gate-crashers and burglars. The ultimate "insider" status is that of being an insider to God. It is inevitable, then, that the world's religions should constitute the major field for the making of outsiders. Which is why religion, far more than politics and economics, continues to feed and give sanction to war.

Luke is a most vigorous champion of the outsider. An outsider himself (the only Gentile in the quartet of Gospel storytellers), he quietly, skillfully, relentlessly, makes it virtually impossible to understand the company of Jesus as an exclusive club. He repeatedly and explicitly brings into the story the very people who are commonly excluded: women, lepers, the racially different (Samaritans), the poor, common laborers (sheepherders), the unfit and the misfit, enemies, and foreigners. He will not countenance Jesus as the patron of a club. His companionship and travels with St. Paul gave him ample opportunity to break into the dominant "clubs" of the first-century world (Roman, Greek, and Jew) and walk away, leaving their doors wide open to the welcome of God in Jesus. Unobtrusively, but effectively, he wrote his experience into the story. The last word in the Greek text of his two-volume story is "unhindered" *(akolutos)*.

St. John

Matthew, Mark, and Luke each employ the same story line in their narrations. But not woodenly or slavishly. Each enjoys a remarkable freedom in the writing; there is no hint that the basic plot either restricts or interferes with their story-making. But John writes the story from a quite different angle. It is recognizably the same story, but the sudden shift of perspective and tone engages us in the narration differently. Novelist John Updike observes that if we view Matthew, Mark, and Luke as progressively sedimentary, John is metamorphic—all the strata violently annealed into something quite different.[6]

John is the final writer both in the sequence in which

we read the Gospel stories in our New Testaments and in the order in which they were written. The early traditions of the church tell us that John wrote as a very old man in his nineties. The traditions also identify him as the apostle most intimate with Jesus while he lived ("the disciple whom Jesus loved"). John's telling of the story fuses the exuberance of a youthful and intense intimacy with Jesus with the sagacious leisure of a centennial life of prayed obedience and love.

We realize the intimacy through conversations. John's storytelling consists primarily of Jesus' conversations. John brings Jesus to us alive on the page through his conversations. John's opening sentence, "In the beginning was the Word . . .", the Word that brought all creation into being and entered our history and lives in the historical flesh-and-blood person of Jesus in first-century Palestine, is elaborated throughout his story as a person who uses words in personal conversations with all sorts and conditions of people, conversations brief and lengthy, conversations pithy and elaborate, but *conversations.* Not declamations to a generalized "world," but person-to-person conversations. The Lord of language uses language not to "lord it over" anyone but to engender relationships of grace and love, creating community and maturing in prayer.

The frequency of Jesus' frequent and justly famous assertion, "I am . . . ," throughout these conversations, makes the story work at two levels (or in two dimensions) simultaneously: it echoes the revelation of God's new name to Moses, "I am . . ." (Exodus 3:14), and it initiates understanding by using the simplest and most accessible diction and grammar, the personal use of the verb *to be.* Jesus' conversations develop and accumulate through this story, conversations between Jesus and his mother, Jesus and his disciples, Jesus and Nicodemus, Jesus and the Samaritan, Jesus and the paralytic, Jesus and the blind, Jesus and the Jews, Jesus and Mary, Jesus and Caiaphas, Jesus and Pilate, and, without any change of tone or diction, Jesus and God. We realize that God is speaking in this voice of Jesus, God's word that called all creation into being, the God who identified himself grammatically ("I am . . .") as the savior of Israel, is again speaking in these conversations—*God's* word. But all these words are ordinary words, words that I can understand, words that I use myself on the street and in the kitchen: bread, birth, water, road, door, light, walking and seeing, believing and loving. There is hardly a word in St. John's storytelling that I have not used myself with comprehension since I have been five years old. We realize that we are included in and are on the edge of becoming participants in these conversations.

Intimacy. Jesus, by means of John's story, invites us into his life, God's life, in terms and in circumstances that are immediately accessible. The simplest grammar is employed to make us participants in this story. John does not try to impress us with big words or highfalutin concepts; he does not flaunt his credentials; he does not bully or intimidate with a show of authority. He renders Jesus in conversation with the same kinds of people we talk to most days, and many of whom we recognize in ourselves.

And leisure. John is a most leisurely storyteller. He takes his time, he repeats, he circles back upon himself. He uses words lovingly, savoring them. Or he holds a sentence up to the light and then rearranges the words, sometimes only slightly, to shift the angle of refraction and bring out another color. Austin Farrer characterizes John's style in this regard as "divinatory brooding."[7] The brisk narrative pace so pronounced in his three story-telling predecessors slows to a meditative Sunday stroll in John.

Edward Dahlberg, in trying to recover Thoreau's prophetic bite for us, insisted that *"Walden* cannot be rushed into men's hearts . . . Persuade and hint."[8] And if Thoreau's *Walden* cannot, how much less can John's Gospel. To read this story, to *heart-listen* to this story, John's millions of appreciative readers have slowed themselves to John's pace, submitting to the tidal rhythms of the conversations, rejecting time-saving doctrinal summaries that tell us what John *means* theologically, without going to all the trouble of listening to him say it. We are not in John's storytelling company long before we realize that he is not nearly as interested in telling us anything new *about* Jesus (although he also does plenty of that along the way) as he is in drawing us into an increasingly intimate relationship *with* Jesus. *Believe* and *love* are his characteristic verbs; neither can be accomplished in a hurry.

And so John gets the final storytelling word. As generation followed generation, there was danger of the story's being reduced to mere history on the one hand or mere doctrine on the other. John renews the original quality of person, of words put to the service of love and belief. Robert Browning's poem "A Death in the Desert," called by William Temple "the most penetrating interpretation of St. John in the English language,"[9] has John, accounting for why he wrote his Jesus story the way he did, say,

> . . . *truth, deadened of its absolute blaze,*
> *Might need love's eye to pierce the o'restretched*
> *doubt.*[10]

John supplies "love's eye." To this day, whenever the brightness of the Jesus story is dulled by depersonalized study or fogged in by cultural stereotypes, John's story is the Gospel of choice to penetrate to the original blaze.

Merkabah Mysticism and Gospel Storytelling

I am using the "Gospel quartet" image to account for

the remarkable congeniality of these four storytellers—each telling his own story in his own voice and yet keeping easy, harmonious company with the others. Other images have been used from time to time to hold Matthew, Mark, Luke, and John in company with one another: the four seasons of the year, four aspects of grammar, four dimensions of time, four points of the compass.

But the most influential image in the early centuries of the church's life derives from Ezekiel's vision of the four cherubim, winged angel-like figures that compose the Throne of God (Ezekiel 1). The four figures are identical except for their faces, which are, respectively, the face of a man (or angel), a lion, an ox, and an eagle. This is the vision that inaugurates Ezekiel's prophetic commission: there is a message to be preached, commissioned by God from his authoritative and sovereign throne.

This image was later picked up in St. John's vision of God seated on his cherubim-throne exercising his rule towards and on the earth, seen and proclaimed as sovereign through John's prophetic message to his churches (Revelation 4-5).

Ireneaus (second century) is the earliest writer to associate the four Gospels with the faces of Ezekiel's cherubim. By the time of Augustine and Jerome (fourth century) the images had taken hold. The Lion, Man, Ox, and Eagle have continued to show up ever since in Christian art, architecture, and exposition. The assignment of particular "faces" to each of the four evangelists always seemed a bit arbitrary and forced. Not uncharacteristically, Calvin was cool to the idea: ". . . in this fiction there is no stability."[11] But the usefulness of the imagery has never been in providing a characteristic feature to each evangelist so much as to connect the four together with the Throne-Cherubim.[12]

The Throne-Cherubim, wildly extravagant, surging

with light and energy, are now the four Gospels, the new Cherubim composing the throne from which God reveals himself and rules. These four Cherubim-Gospels provide the intensely alive and mysteriously indescribable setting from which God's sovereign and saving message is proclaimed. Individually and collectively, these Gospels are the Throne Room of the Sovereign God. These stories will raise the dead and establish the kingdom.

Meanwhile, as Christians were using the cherubim figures as Gospel icons, a Jewish spiritual movement that has come to be known as *merkabah* mysticism was putting them to a very different use. *Merkabah* is the Hebrew word for "chariot." In ancient imagery, the cherubim were associated with a royal/divine chariot, which they pulled across the sky. Royal thrones often were depicted with cherubim arms: the cherubim-throne reflects the basis for the dominion of the king.[13]

In Ezekiel's vision, this chariot-throne was no fixed, static piece of royal furniture but in perpetual, swift movement, capable of seeing and discerning everything, dazzlingly light-filled. God's rule did not operate as a detached judicial decree, but *invaded* the disorder and anarchy of human sin, surprisingly and unpredictably.

The strategies of merkabah mysticism were designed to provide entrance to and participation in the chariot-throne vision—recover the ecstasies, experience the very core of divinity. Intense study, ascetic meditation, withdrawal from everydayness, and an accumulation of esoteric lore were employed to facilitate this experience.

Mysticism, as such, is nothing other than the conviction that God can be, and should be, experienced. "Taste and see that the Lord is good" (Psalm 34:8) is the justifying text for all mysticism. We are not content to know about God cerebrally or collect evidence of God historically. We are not content to be mere spectators to it; most of us want to get in on God personally. Insofar as we conduct our lives to that end we are mystics.

But not infrequently "mystic" acquires a bad odor among Christians when men and women, impatient with (or ignorant of) God's ways of descending to and entering our lives, develop their own ways of ascending to and entering God. Unfortunately, mysticism, this conviction of the possibility and desire for the actuality of experiencing the divine in the human condition, then results in strategies of intensification of the invisible and the private, withdrawing from the visible and the historical. The strategy is to become less human/material/earthly so that you can become more divine/spiritual/heavenly. "Experience" then becomes self-defined, and, often, self-indulgent. The "god" ascended to and entered does not seem to have much to do with the God revealed in Jesus Christ. Obedience, after all, is as much an "experience" as a vision. Carrying another's burden is just as much an "experience" as levitation. The so-called "dark night" is just as much an experience as ecstasy. So however much we admire the spiritual athleticism of some people, and even envy their "insider" stories, we are cautious about embracing them as guides. Merkabah mysticism is one of the early and premier forms of a mysticism that cultivated the inner as opposed to the outer. Gershom Scholem, the greatest of all students of Jewish mysticism, is severe in his judgment. Assessing merkabah mysticism, he wrote, "All its originality is on the ecstatical side, while the moral aspect is starved, so to speak, of life. The moral doctrines . . . are pale and bloodless."[14]

There is no documentary evidence that the Jewish merkabah mystics and the Christian storytellers were aware of each other, but they very likely developed more or less side by side, using the identical Ezekiel vision, though each in their own way.[15] While the Jews were using the vision in esoteric, subjectival ways, pulling their adepts out of the ordinary, the Christians were using the same vision in public, revelational ways, as a vehicle, a "throne" of energy and movement, expressed in the cherubim faces of Lion, Man, Ox, and Eagle, to launch Jesus into the world.

The contrast (and criticism) could not be stronger: By assigning the four cherubim faces to the four evangelists, Christians made the four Gospel storytellers the throne room from which God's sovereignty was expressed. We do not, in other words, get in on the dynamics of God's sovereignty by cultivating esoteric ecstasies but by telling and listening to Jesus stories. The chariot throne from which God's sovereignty issues is composed of the four Gospels.

Christian spirituality, in contrast to merkabah mysticism, consists of Christians sitting around telling and listening to Jesus stories: *this* is the throne from which God reigns; *this* is the center from which his sovereignty develops: personal, relational, discursive *Jesus*. Instead of withdrawing from everydayness and materiality, from flesh and bone, the Christians plunged deeper into it. The four Throne-Cherubim Gospels are not an esoteric state into which we withdraw but vehicles that we ride into the thick of God's inaugurated kingdom. Along the way there are also ecstasies, but they are footnotes to the story, not its plot. *Gospel* is a story-ing verb, not an abstract state.

Words, as such, do not make anything happen. It is the *way* they are used—context and syntax, grammatical mood and poetic rhythm—that provides the meaning. *God* out of context, without syntax, can be either blessing or blasphemy. Story-less talk and writing is a blight on our world in general these days, but most damagingly on the world of Christian discourse. Happily, though, there are numerous springs in the desert where our devout storytellers (writers and pastors and singers) are at work in the gospel way, keeping our imaginations story-trained, our lives story-responsive, so that we are still capable of praying to our Lord, *"Gospel* me to the Garden."

Author Biography

Eugene H. Peterson is professor of spiritual theology at Regent College in Vancouver, B.C. A pastor, poet, scholar, preacher, and teacher, Peterson is the translator of *The Message* (his new rendering of the Bible) and the author of many books, including *Living the Message, Reversed Thunder, Answering God,* and *Leap Over a Wall.* He is a member of the Chrysostom Society and lives in Montana.

Back when I was still struggling to become a writer for children, my own children, who were great fans, urged me to read *A Wrinkle in Time.* Since then I have had the pleasure of being on several conference programs with Ms. L'Engle and reading many L'Engle books, but I have yet to catch up with my daughter Mary, who at last count had read *A Ring of Endless Light* eighteen times.

Katherine Paterson

6
Taking the Bible Seriously*

Katherine Paterson

Years ago I was teaching Bible in a Methodist prep school where most of the students had never read the Bible and were doing so now only under extreme duress. Put simply, they could not graduate unless they passed my course. That did not mean they had to like the course. Indeed, hardly a day went by that one of them did not protest the foolishness of what they were being required to read—the uselessness for modern life. How could any intelligent person be expected to take the Bible seriously? It was just a bunch of myths and not very good ones at that. On one particular day we were discussing the chaotic last days of the Northern Kingdom. In the fifteenth chapter of 2 Kings, you may recall, Zechariah is assassinated by Shallam, and Shallam is killed in turn by Menahen, who despite all his wickedness seems to die a natural death, but his son Pekiah is slaughtered by his captain Pekah, who in turn is assassinated by Hoshea, who is eventually disposed of by the Assyrians who have conquered the land.

Before we had gotten halfway through this litany of

civil disaster, the boys were furious. "Look at that," one student spoke out for the rest. "This is ridiculous—all those crazy Israelites supposedly killing off all their kings. Why are we wasting time studying this, anyway?"

I never answered his question, for at that moment, the classroom door flew open, and the history professor burst in, his face white with horror, "Someone just shot the President!" he said.

There were no more vocal complaints from my students that term, although I do not think I was ever quite able to convince them to take the Bible seriously. But those teenagers are not so different from most adults I meet, who find it incomprehensible that I still take the Bible seriously. "Okay, so your parents were missionaries, but haven't you outgrown that stuff by now?" There is also a notion that one could not possibly be both a good writer and a good Christian.

There is further confusion when my books are attacked, most often by my fellow Christians who do not believe that I take the Bible seriously enough. One student at a Christian college took me to task for wanting to pick out of the Bible those parts I considered important and let the rest go. "You have to believe and obey the whole Word of God," he said. "But we don't," I protested. "I don't think any of us do. Do you obey the dietary laws of Leviticus? I surely don't."

"We don't have to obey the dietary laws," he said. "We have freedom in Christ."

"Exactly."

And implicit in that freedom, as Madeleine L'Engle teaches us in *Penguins and Golden Calves,* is the ability to see the Bible as an icon rather than an idol—a window to God rather than an object of worship.

At the risk of losing readers when I have hardly begun this essay, I am going to put in a plug for Christian mythology. We need, I believe, to recapture the word *myth* when we speak about the Bible. The *Oxford Eng-*

lish Dictionary defines myth as "a purely fictitious narrative usually involving supernatural persons, actions, or events, and embodying some popular idea concerning natural or historical phenomena" or "a fictitious or imaginary person or object."

These definitions are the ones my students had, and they are the ones in common use today, but with all due respect to the *OED*, it is totally misleading to think of myth in such terms. We would be much closer to the meaning of myth if we thought of it in Madeleine L'Engle's terms, as icon, as window through which we see truth.

Or take the Japanese definition. In my English-Japanese dictionary, myth is translated as *shinwa,* written as two Chinese characters, the first, *shin,* is the character for God or god (both singular and plural), the second, *wa,* means talk, story, tale, fable, news, rumor, consultation—a rich word indeed. A myth is, therefore, Godtalk, Godstory, maybe even Godnews. Now we are getting close to the old English Godspell or Gospel. This is a definition of myth that suits me beautifully, but before I take it and run, I am obliged to consult the experts. In his book on the Bible entitled *The Great Code,* Northrop Frye designates as myth those narratives which a particular society has "charged with a special seriousness and importance."[1]

Thus, a myth is a story that contains knowledge that is important for the functioning of a certain society, but, as we have often seen, it also contains elements that are universal, elements that apply to many human situations. Most myths also have to do, as the Japanese word reminds us, with Godstory or godstories. Every human society seems to have a longing for stories that tell us why the universe is as it is, and why we are as we are— stories that give our short lives on earth an eternal dimension. "I want to know," Albert Einstein once said, "I want to know how God created this world. I am not interested in this or that phenomenon. I want to know His thoughts, the rest are details.[2]

But a myth is not simply an explanatory tale; it is, as Joseph Campbell reminds us, a story in which the hearers take part. "The life of a mythology," he says, "derives from the vitality of its symbols as metaphors delivering, not simply the idea, but a sense of actual participation."[3]

So the Bible is not only myth in Frye's definition as knowledge that "is important for a society to know," but it has also, as Campbell says a mythology must, provided to peoples over the ages and around the world the sense of actual participation in the mythic events retold in its pages. Take, for example, the story of the Exodus:

When Israel was in Egypt's land,
Let my people go!
Oppressed so hard they could not stand,
Let my people go!
Go down, Moses, way down in Egypt's land,
Tell old Pharaoh,
Let my people go!

This song was written and first sung by people who were not Hebrews and had never seen Egypt. But they were people who knew what oppression was and so metaphorically participated in the pain of Egyptian bondage and the living hope that God would send them a Moses-like deliverer.

And in the eighth century, John of Damascus wrote a great Easter hymn which relates the resurrection of Christ to the Exodus.

Come, ye faithful, raise the strain
Of triumphant gladness;
God hath brought forth Israel
Into joy from sadness;
Loosed from Pharaoh's bitter yoke

Jacob's sons and daughters;
Led them, with unmoistened foot,
Through the Red Sea waters.

The virgin forests of the new world in no way resembled
the Sinai desert, but still for the early European settlers,
America was both the biblical wilderness and the Promised Land. They named their cities, New Canaan, Bethel,
Bethany, Salem, Goshen, bringing the biblical myth to
flower in new soil. Tragedy resulted when they claimed
themselves to be the children of promise and drove out
the inhabitants of the land as the Israelites had done in
the original Canaan almost 3000 years before.

Indeed, the myth of the Hebrew exodus from Egyptian captivity, the parting of the Red Sea waters, the journey, the giving of the law at Sinai, the entrance across
the River Jordan into the Promised Land of Canaan has
been the source of powerful symbols for many people
who long for freedom and homelands. It is only a two-
hundred-mile trip from Egypt to Canaan, but the children of Israel, because of the sin of distrust, wandered
for forty years in the wilderness of Sinai led by a pillar
of cloud by day and a pillar of fire by night, fed by the
mysterious manna which God gave from heaven, their
thirst quenched by water which gushed from the rock
struck by Moses. I could go on and on, but all these
powerful elements of the myth come down to us and
have become a part of our ordinary language. "It's not
written in stone," we say, in oblique reference to those
ten laws that were.

The mythology of the Bible no longer dominates our
Western consciousness as it once did. I was quite aware
of this fact just after *Jacob Have I Loved* was published.
"What is the name of your new book?" people would
ask. *"Jacob Have I Loved,"* I would answer and the face
of my questioner would go blank. Only once do I recall
giving the title of the book and having the questioner

fill in the rest of the quotation: "But Esau have I hated." And that person, knowing the Genesis story, already knew what the novel was about; he did not need to ask.

But most people do not know the biblical stories, and those of us who do often have problems sorting out what the stories mean for us. In a world where waters do not part to let us cross with unmoistened foot, and rocks in the desert do not gush forth water, how are we to perceive such stories? As fairy tale, as nonsense, or as the bread of life? At the trial of Jesus, Pilate, the Roman governor, says to Jesus, "What is truth?" Earlier in the Gospel of John, the evangelist quotes Jesus as saying to his friend Thomas, "I am the way, the truth, and the life," but when the question is put to Jesus at his trial by the secular authority who has the power to put him to death, Jesus does not answer, perhaps because he knew that the man would not know a metaphor from a menorah.

What is truth? We live in a world where truth is often equated with fact—and fact is that which can be scientifically verified in a laboratory. Myth becomes then—in the *OED* definition of the word—"a purely fictitious narrative." Metaphor is merely a figure of speech, sometimes more apt or clever than other times, but hardly life-changing.

We can look back with respect to an earlier time when truth was determined not in the laboratory but in the forum and in the record. In those days, reasoned argument could reveal truth, as could the written historical account. But we look back, if not with disdain, with a certain knowing amusement, to the naive days of old when truth was carried about in story—in the myths of the society, in the shinwa, in the Godstory.

Northrop Frye sees these three ages of truth-telling as three phases of language. There is the ancient metaphorical phase, which is poetic and speaks of many gods in language that is concrete. In the age of mythology,

there is potential magic in any metaphorical use of
words. The second age of language began, perhaps, with
Plato and his intellectual contemporaries. Here language
became abstract. God became an idea and an ideal that
one could discuss, not God, a person one could tell
stories about. God was no longer Yahweh or Zeus but
the Form of the Good or the Unmoved Mover. In this
age God was no longer directly active in the affairs of
humankind. God was a transcendent idea. This kind of
language about God existed right down to the nineteenth century, when suddenly God was not so much
declared dead as dismissed as irrelevant.

Incidentally, this is when Christian fundamentalism
began. It is a relatively late arrival in Christian thought.
In earlier days, there had been no argument about
whether the stories of the Bible were literal, factual, able
to be verified in a laboratory. Nobody really thought in
those terms. Indeed, most of biblical interpretation employed a kind of typology. As an example, *The Song of
Songs* can be taken at face value as a quite earthy love
song with rather amazing figures of speech:

> How beautiful you are, my love,
>   how very beautiful!
> Your eyes are doves
>   behind your veil. . . .
> Your teeth are like a flock of shorn ewes
>   that have come up from the washing,
> all of which bear twins. . . .
> Your neck is like the tower of David,
>   built in courses;
> on it hang a thousand bucklers,
>   all of them shields of warriors.[4]

Instead of regarding the Hebrew poem as a secular love
song, which it probably was, the early church Fathers
saw it as a song about the love of Christ for the church,

91

but nobody considered that a woman's eyes were literally doves any more than that her neck was an actual battle tower.

The dietary and ceremonial laws of the Hebrew Bible were thought to be no longer binding on Christians because they were "allegories of the spiritual truth of the Gospel."[5] Everything in the Old Testament was a type, a sort of a foretelling of the New, and everything in the New was to fulfill the Old.

The Bible itself sometimes plays fast and loose with historical events and romps through contradictory statements within a few verses of each other. It delights in hyperbole, abounds in parables, allegories, and poetic imagery. Perhaps no book in history has had so many editors, but there was not a responsible copy editor in the lot. And nobody was much bothered by this until the late nineteenth century.

It was only when fact became that which was scientifically verifiable, and fact became the opposite of fiction, and myth stopped being the knowledge that was important for a society and became, instead, a "purely fictitious narrative," that earnest Christians, seeking to defend the Bible as "true," began to insist that a prophet named Jonah was actually in the belly of a large fish for three days, and to pin their faith on the ruins of a huge and mysterious vessel purported to be on top of a mountain in Turkey, and to deny evidence of any process that would suggest the world as we know it had been more than six calendar days in the making, and to try to explain away the apparent errors of fact and self-contradictory statements that the biblical writers and editors cheerfully left standing in the text. In short, it has only been in the last hundred years or so that Christians have felt a need to maintain that every word of the book they call the Word of God be taken literally—and regarded as fact in the same way a chemical experiment in a laboratory is regarded as fact.

Meantime, Einstein was born and grew to maturity, and now our wise men and women tell us that what appears to be substantial is illusion—that matter is energy, or spirit, if you will—that there may be not the three dimensions of our senses, but that there may very well be parallel universes, time warps, and ten or more dimensions. And our most brilliant scientists speak in poetic metaphors because the language of our age, which is still the language of Newton and his contemporaries, is not up to the task of relating the ideas that today's scientific imaginations are wrestling with.

The Christian Bible, as you know, is not one book, but a sort of library, now separated into sixty-six books written over a period of well over a thousand years and in at least three languages. The earliest portions of the Bible come from the metaphorical age—so that we have, for example, the assumption of multiple gods in the song of Moses celebrating the passage across the Red Sea.

Who is like you, O Lord, among the gods?
Who is like you, majestic in holiness,
awesome in splendor, doing wonders?[6]

We have, as well, a very human sort of Olympian figure who smells the "sweet savor" of Noah's sacrificial altar and says in his heart, "I will never again curse the ground because of humankind."[7] We have the wonderful stories of Abraham arguing with God face to face over the fate of Sodom, and Jacob wrestling with the mysterious figure who turns out to be sometimes an angel, sometimes God himself.

But the Bible is written over such a long period of time that we see in it changing or evolving beliefs about God and changes in the language with which it speaks about God. In the prophets, God is no longer perceived as the one walking in the garden at the cool of the day, smelling the sacrifice, ordering the slaughter of all who would dare oppose his chosen people. God is seen as transcendent and one, not an Olympian figure among a pantheon of gods and goddesses. Nor does he (and in the Bible God is pretty consistently referred to as "he" not "she," "it," or "they") confine his concerns to a single nation. The tribal deity of early Israel has become the ruler of all the earth and the heavens as well. The tribal deities of other nations are no gods at all. They are merely idols of wood, stone, and metal made by human hands. The prophet of the Babylonian exile, also called Second Isaiah, says: "Thus says the Lord, the King of Israel, and his Redeemer, the Lord of hosts: I am the first and I am the last; besides me there is no god."[8]

The Jewish prophets are a unique phenomenon in the annals of religion. We think of prophets as foretelling the future, and in that sense there were plenty of those around. But the prophets whose lives and messages have been preserved through the Bible are less concerned about the future than they are about the present of their own time. Some of them spoke out against idolatry and against the dangers of embracing the false gods of the neighboring tribes and nations, but when we get to persons such as Isaiah and Jeremiah and Amos, they were far less interested in purity of religion than they were in justice.

Amos the herdsman stands before the golden calves of the shrine at Bethel, but he does not preach against the idolatry of the calves. In his declaration of God's message, he cries,

> Hear this, you that trample on the needy,
> and bring to ruin the poor of the land,
> saying, "When will the new moon be over
> so that we may sell grain;
> and the sabbath,
> so that we may offer wheat for sale?
> We will make the ephah small and the shekel great,

and practice deceit with false balances,
buying the poor for silver
and the needy for a pair of sandals,
and selling the sweepings of the wheat."[9]

I hate, I despise your festivals,
and I take no delight in your solemn
assemblies.
Even though you offer me your burnt offerings
and grain offerings,
I will not accept them;
and the offerings of well-being of your fatted
animals
I will not look upon.
Take away from me the noise of your songs;
I will not listen to the melody of your harps.
But let justice roll down like waters,
and righteousness like an ever-flowing stream.[10]

Among the thundering voices of judgment, crying out
the Lord's demand for justice, there is also among the
prophets a quiet voice of infinite mercy. The people may
sin, they may go away from God, but God will never
cease to love them.

In the book of Hosea, the word of the Lord sounds
more like the word of a loving mother:

When Israel was a child, I loved him,
and out of Egypt I called my son.
The more I called them,
the more they went from me;
they kept sacrificing to the Baals,
and offering incense to idols.

Yet it was I who taught Ephraim to walk,
I took them up in my arms;
but they did not know that I healed them.

I led them with cords of human kindness,
   with bands of love.
I was to them like those
   who lift infants to their cheeks.
   I bent down to them and fed them. . . .

How can I give you up, Ephraim?
   How can I hand you over, O Israel?
How can I make you like Admah?
   How can I treat you like Zeboiim?
My heart recoils within me;
   my compassion grows warm and tender.
I will not execute my fierce anger;
   I will not again destroy Ephraim;
for I am God and no mortal,
   the Holy One in your midst,
   and I will not come in wrath.[11]

In the latter part of the book of Isaiah, another new figure appears—a servant of God, an anointed one—who comes not as a king to conquer but as a servant of all. Now the Jews did not have our obsession with the individual. The servant sometimes seems to be the whole nation of Israel, or the remnant of the nation that would return after the exile in Babylon. God's anointed servant is sometimes not a Jew at all; Cyrus, the king of Persia, who defeated the hated Babylonians and let the Jews return home, is also called God's servant. He is even spoken of as God's anointed one (which is what *Messiah* means). Sometimes the servant seems to be a mystical individual. Anyhow the Servant in Second Isaiah jars the notion of what it means to be the chosen one of God.

For he [the servant] grew up before him [the
   Lord] like a young plant,
   and like a root out of dry ground;

he had no form or majesty that we should look
at him,
nothing in his appearance that we should
desire him.
He was despised and rejected by others;
a man of suffering and acquainted with
infirmity;
and as one from whom others hide their faces
he was despised, and we held him of no
account.

Surely he has borne our infirmities
and carried our diseases;
yet we accounted him stricken,
struck down by God, and afflicted.
But he was wounded for our transgressions,
crushed for our iniquities;
upon him was the punishment that made us
whole,
and by his bruises we are healed.
All we like sheep have gone astray;
we have all turned to our own way,
and the Lord has laid on him the iniquity of us
all.[12]

There is also in the prophets the notion that Israel, the
figure of the anointed servant, has been chosen by God
not for special privileges but to bring the world to a
new age, a messianic kingdom:

It is too light a thing that you should be my
servant
to raise up the tribes of Jacob
and to restore the survivors of Israel;
I will give you as a light to the nations,
that my salvation may reach to the end of the
earth.[13]

This messianic kingdom, which the prophets imagined and portrayed in joyful and glowing detail, would be a time of peace and prosperity, not only for the Jews, but for all peoples, all birds and beasts, all nature, all the earth.

Jesus is seen in the Gospel stories as fulfilling the hopes of the prophets. In the book of Luke we read that he goes to the synagogue in Nazareth, his home town, and the local fathers ask him to take part in the service. They hand him the scroll of Isaiah to read aloud and Jesus finds the place where the prophet, writing about the Servant, says: "The Spirit of the Lord is upon me, because he has anointed me to bring good news to the poor.

"He has sent me to proclaim release to the captives and recovery of sight to the blind, to let the oppressed go free, to proclaim the year of the Lord's favor."

Jesus' commentary on the passage is short and direct. "Today," he says, "this scripture has been fulfilled in your hearing."[14]

And that is what New Testament shinwa, Godspell, myth is all about—the Godstory of the Hebrew Scriptures culminating, coming to fruition, in the person of Jesus of Nazareth.

This makes the Bible a unique sort of writing. The theological term for it is the Greek word *kerygma*, which means "proclamation" and is often equated with "gospel." The shinwa of the Bible, whether we speak of the Hebrew or Christian Bible, is not, as Frye reminds us, metaphorical literature, though it certainly has metaphorical elements. Nor is it transcendent, rational, allegorical, historical, descriptive, or objective literature. Even though it contains all those elements in varying degrees, the language neither of the Hebrew Bible nor the Christian New Testament "coincides" with any of the three phases of language with which history is familiar. The Bible cannot be read simply metaphorically or allegorically, and certainly not descriptively or literally—the way, for example, that you would read a contemporary work of non-fiction. The Godstory of the Bible is intended to be *revelation.*

And what precisely does it seek to reveal? Not that God is. It begins with that assumption. It seeks to reveal the action of God in the human story, and it does this in the language of love. As Frye says, "The *kerygma,* or proclaiming rhetoric, of the Bible is a welcoming and approaching rhetoric. . . . Coming the other way is the body of human imaginative response, as we have it in literature and the arts."[15]

I think Frye is onto something here. I had never heard it articulated just this way before, but there is something in the vast and varied and yet mysteriously unified language of the Bible that welcomes human response. Look at the response it has received in art, music, literature through the centuries, though in the second half of this century what response there has been seems to have manifested itself more often in an angry cry of rebellion or a softened, embarrassed whisper. And in those rare instances today when a Christian such as Madeleine L'Engle dares to write openly and joyfully in response to the biblical story, she often finds herself attacked by fellow Christians who have yet to learn the biblical language of love.

But this is nothing new. Frye reminds us that Plato holds up Socrates as the archetypal teacher, and then goes on to construct his own ideal society in which a person like Socrates could not exist. "Similarly, Christianity is founded on a prophet who was put to death as a blasphemer and a social menace, hence any persecuting Christian is assuming that Pilate and Caiaphas were right in principal, and should merely have selected a different victim."[16]

But even the most well meaning can fail to see that a response to the biblical proclamation involves the writer in often painful and unpleasant truths. Not too long ago a child in a school where I was speaking asked me: "When are you going to write a Christian book?"

"I am a Christian," I said, "and I would hope all my books are Christian books, but I think you're asking something else. I think you're asking when I'm going to write a book where nobody cusses and everybody behaves themselves." He nodded solemnly.

"I'm sorry," I said, "but it's not going to happen. In a novel the writer seeks to tell the truth about human nature. I am trying to tell the truth. I do not believe God is honored by lies."

To see only those books which portray exemplary human behavior as Christian is to misunderstand the biblical proclamation. I find this proclamation best articulated in the prophets and in Jesus' embodiment of the prophetic word.

There is freedom in the gospel, a freedom that does not exist when the response to the gospel must be a morally blameless life. None of us is capable of such a life. But when we hear the language of a love that is in no way dependent on our worthiness—a love that is given simply because we have been born and a love that cherishes our uniqueness, our imaginations leap to respond.

The Godstory of the Bible tells me that God's children can argue with their maker. Abraham does, why can't I? So I take the story of Jacob, the twin God chooses, and retell it from the point of view of Esau—the unchosen one. And I find, to my surprised delight, that in Genesis Esau grows up to be a lovely man who forgives his brother and treats him with courtesy and trust. Which is more than Jacob ever does for Esau. There is an old Hasidic saying that shares my affection for Esau. "The Messiah will not come," it says, "until the tears of Esau cease." And this saying, along with the prophetic word of God's universal mercy, says that Esau is loved—that he is not beyond the perimeter of God's tender concern. Nor am I. Nor are you.

This is the proclamation that I was born into, the proclamation that I, like Jacob of old, have wrestled with and clung to all my life, demanding its blessing. This is the knowledge that it is vital for me to know, for without it I do not know who I am. These are the myths—the shinwa—of the people I belong to and choose every day to continue to be a part of. This is the "welcoming and approaching" language of the biblical myth to which my writing and, I pray, all of my life will be a joyful and imaginative response.

Author Biography

Katherine Paterson was born in China, the daughter of Presbyterian missionaries. At the start of World War II, the family returned to the United States and lived in Virginia, North Carolina, and West Virginia until she left for King College in Bristol, Tennessee. In addition to her degree in English literature, which she received from King, Paterson earned master's degrees from the Presbyterian School of Christian Education in Richmond, Virginia, and Union Theological Seminary in New York City. She taught school in rural Virginia and also spent four years as a missionary of the Presbyterian Church, U.S.A., in Japan before marrying a Presbyterian minister. The Patersons have four grown children and four grandchildren.

Katherine Paterson is the author of more than twenty books, including twelve novels for young people. Two of these are National Book Award Winners, *The Master Puppeteer* (1977) and *The Great Gilly Hopkins* (1979). She also received the Newbery Medal in 1978 for *Bridge to Terabithia* and again in 1981 for *Jacob Have I Loved.* Her latest novel is *Jip, His Story,* the winner of the 1997 Scott O'Dell Award for Historical Fiction.

I first met Madeleine L'Engle in 1965, when she (bravely) took me on as a sort of assistant director for a Christmas pageant at the Cathedral of St. John the Divine in New York.

One did not have to be around Madeleine long before one was aware (electrically aware, if there is such a phrase allowable) that here was a woman of more than routine interest, to borrow *The New Yorker*'s phrase. Here was an imagination that seemed to know no limits. Here was a grasp of, and a love for, the knobbly, tangy, maddening, exhilarating texture of our mortal life, perched as it is on the cusp between the seen and the unseen.

Over the years, Madeleine and her husband, Hugh, became good friends of ours. We mourned his death with her. We also (this "we" is my family and I) owe her a debt: her work, along with that of T. S. Eliot and Flannery O'Connor, was a *(the?)* mainstay of our daughter's faith during her years at Harvard. So we thank God for Madeleine L'Engle.

Thomas Howard

7

Of Imagination, Story, and Reality

Thomas Howard

We find, often, a breakdown between those on the one hand whose approach to God and the world is propositionalist, syllogistic, discursive, and verbalist, and those on the other hand who find themselves reaching for the vocabulary of myth, image, and sacrament as they try to grapple with what matters about the universe. The vocabulary of the two parties differs. The philosophers sometimes suspect that the poets believe in elves.

That raises a piquant question: What about elves? The peril here is of finding that the whole discussion has got suddenly frivolous.

Such a question (whatever the question is about elves) does give immediacy and color, we might say, to the sort of thing we approach when we speak of myth and reality. It has to do with one's stance, or posture, in the world. One man, for example, if you asked him about elves, might snort, "That's rubbish. There aren't, and never have been, any such creatures." This man knows a very great deal, and is quite brisk about shutting down various ontological shutters, we might say. Another man, if asked, might say, "Elves? Well—if there ever were such beings, not only do we know nothing about them: their story, if there is any such story, has nothing to do with our story, at least not yet." This man may have an entirely businesslike outlook on things, and would not be caught dead joining hobbit societies, or naming his dog Frodo, or turning over cabbage leaves looking for leprechauns. The borders of his metaphysical imagination, however, are indeterminate. Mists obscure the frontiers of his world. Reality for him, eventually, reaches over the hills and far away. He may be as earthy, precise, and unsentimental when it comes to sticking to quotidian reality as, say, John Knox or St. Joseph the Carpenter; but his world spreads out into mystery, and his awareness of mystery is not exhausted by his giving a merely ontological or theological nod in the direction of that which transcends our grasp. For him, the world really is suffused with mystery, and the leaves of reality rustle and whisper with rumor. There is fear in a handful of dust for him. Angelic and demonic footfalls really do echo along the corridors of the universe for him. He lives in a world where the morning stars have been known to sing, or to fight against Sisera, or to point astrologers to the birthplace of an incarnate deity. He is less sure of what is not going on than he is of what is going on. If the sons of god come in to the daughters of men, or gigantic Anakim stride across the landscape of Mesopotamia, or dead bodies show up in the streets of Jerusalem on the afternoon of Pontius Pilate, he will not be the one to scoff. And as for elves—well, they are certainly there, fugitive and evanescent, at least in the stories that have flickered unremittingly and immemorially along the borders of the narratives told in every tribe and culture since the expulsion from Eden.

In this connection we may recall the story which is unfurled in the Bible. We understand that story to be true in some sense which outstrips the myths—the tales, that is, which we find being told amongst the Babylonians and Egyptians and Greeks and Norsemen. We hear the tale of Adam and Eve, for example, and we receive it as true, whereas we hear about Yggdrasil and Ginnungagap, or about Chronos and Zeus, and we demur: such tales, while they strike haunting chords in our souls, and seem to arise from the very wellspring of things, are not "true" in the sense in which the story of Eden is true.

There are problems here. We all know about literary forms, certainly, and many ferociously orthodox Christians might wish to be allowed room to speculate when it comes to taking up a point of view as to whether Adam and Eve were one man and one woman in a garden as we know gardens. When we get to these early and misty regions in the story of our world, we tread more and more gingerly. Who knows what was going on, or how to visualize it all? We believe the story, indeed; but is the story exactly the same sort of account of things as we find in the newspaper account of an event, or the description in a history text of the battles along the Somme in World War I?

Let us for the moment lean towards the ditch on the "literal" side of the question here. That is, in thinking of the huge mystery that shrouds the story of Adam and Eve, with the Lord God taking a rib out of the man, or walking in the garden in the cool of the day—in thinking of such a scenario, may we ask whether, if TV cameras had been hidden in the ferns of Eden, would they have yielded footage of a magnificent naked man stretched out on the moss in a deep slumber, and of hands opening up the skin of his torso and breaking off a rib? Then presently, on camera, a naked woman coming into being right there?

But now we are all embarrassed. Come, do not speak to us of TV footage and of Eden in the same breath.

Is not our embarrassment over this clumsy juxtaposition of ancient Creation narrative and modern technology—is not this embarrassment an index of our anguished awareness that we are onlookers at events which arrive on our stage from the precincts of everlasting deity? They are events which burst the boundaries of our powers, and also of the power of words. What is human language to do when it finds itself asked to report, or at least to intimate, such events?

At the deepest levels of our being we seem to be aware of a property of ineffability which suffuses such events, and which challenges language to the utmost. We do not know quite what to do at such a juncture. We have mythic language: shall we roll out the machinery of myth as perhaps the only equipment we have by way of mediating the ineffable to our sorely limited powers of understanding? Or will eyewitness news do the trick?

The point, of course, is simply that we do not know how to visualize Eden, and since the story tells it with such and such a texture, we will not go far wrong by sticking fairly close to that texture.

But is it not just a sort of bravado, or derring-do, which inclines us to stick close to the texture of the Genesis narrative, as over against the post-Enlightenment proclivity for fraying out, or teasing out, the dense and knotty warp and woof of that narrative into a looser skein of indeterminate stuff? In the tight fabric of the story that Genesis is pleased to give us, we have those two people pacing the stage. In the looser skein preferred by our own epoch, we have aeons of time, and gradualness, and perhaps primates passing from Cro-Magnon to Piltdown to Neanderthal to *Pithecanthropus Erectus,* and then some universal misstep on the part of these creatures in a calamity which we may call the Fall. And even to imagine such a calamity is, really, primarily to testify to our own unhappy conviction that something is deeply amiss in our world and in our mortal experience. Something is rotten in the state of Denmark. This cannot be right. Well, then: let us turn to these ancient tales that arose during the earliest stages of our human self-awareness, and seize upon them, and keep them alive, and look upon them as vivid and trenchant ways of recording our own deepest hunches about things.

In the light of such a discussion we find ourselves asking what we think reality is like. The closer we can make our language approximate reality, the better off we are, we say. Is reality more like the fundamentalist Garden of Eden, with ferns and palms and murmuring brooks, or is it more like the diffuse generalities and developments summoned by talk of gradualness and evolution and scarcely perceptible aeonian movements? Did we mortals fall on some unhappy Thursday morning at about 11:45, just before lunch? Or is it that we are profoundly aware of some tragic disjuncture at the very root of our humanity which stems from—from who knows what?

Must a choice be made between the two? That is, is reality such that we have some categorical reason for disallowing the fundamentalist ferns and insisting upon a truth which is more nearly approached by the language of generality? How do we know that the ferns supply "only" a picture? What is it that we have found out about reality in our latter day which obliges us to translate that child's garden of narrative in Genesis out into the propositions and generalities commonly brought into play in such disciplines as anthropology, biblical studies, and archaeology?

From the Christian point of view, reality is not far from being synonymous with "the eternal." It is what is. But what is it like? There's the rub. And we all have to confess straight off that it is impossible to raise this topic without calling into play our imaginations, since we are such creatures as want a picture of what we are talking about.

But then we find ourselves divided: on the one hand

our imagination busily cobbles up pictures for us and offers them to our thinking; but on the other, another property in us warns us away from the pictures, whispering, "Steady now. You know that that is only a picture, and that the reality you are thinking about isn't really like that. You'll get closer to the truth if you keep those pictures where they belong, namely, penned up in a pen called 'Fancy.'" One part of us inclines to caper out over picturesque hills and valleys while we think, and another part summons us to stay serious, and stick with the imagery of abstraction, or the categorical, or the propositional.

I have used the word *imagery* in connection with the words *abstraction* and so forth. For of course how we think of those abstractions is itself pictorial. For most of us the abstract is wider, and thinner, and emptier than is the imagistic, and we try to keep it as colorless as our powers will permit. We think we are being more serious, that is, closer to the truth, in so far as our mind is not depending on pictures. Pictures take us over towards the neighborhood of fancy, while abstractions place us firmly in serious discourse.

But is this axiomatic? Do we, in fact, set story aside and reach for the vocabulary of abstract proposition as we struggle to get closer to reality?

Christianity and Judaism before it do not allow us to settle for the gnostic notion that "real" reality is vacuous, and that matter is to be regretted. Obviously we have to do our thinking about reality in the light of what presents itself to our powers, and what presents itself to us is blue sky and blue water and green grass and green trees and red tulips and red strawberries.

Oh-ho, says our gnostic friend. You've just given me the game. Those properties you just listed are in your perceptions, not in the sky and the grass and the strawberries.

This is a nettlesome topic. But Christianity, at least,

would proceed upon a set of suppositions that constitutes a sort of backdrop, or better, a pavement, for all the rest of our suppositions.

First, we have a Creation that presents itself to us. All of us, gnostics and hard-core sacramentalists, would agree that what we have here is rock and water and fern and thrushes and wheat and grapes. It is all very solid. Even the so-called intangibles like the song of the hermit thrush, are, when you come down to it, material, since it takes the bird's little throat membranes, and air waves, and your ear drum membranes to get the song. The Creation presents itself to us thus.

And it presents itself, secondly, to *us*. What are we? We are not angels who, they tell us, can perceive reality directly, unfiltered through eardrums and retinas and olfactory nerves and taste buds and fingertips. The reality of Creation is mediated to us via our taste buds and so forth. A corollary from the Christian point of view here would be that it is mediated in some sense faithfully and not fraudulently. Christians believe in the trustworthiness of Creation, since we attribute trustworthiness to the Creator. All the blueness and greenness and sweetness and wetness and tang and bite and solidity of it all testifies in some sense truthfully to the One who made it.

But who, or what, are we? We are creatures made for this Creation, or rather, for whom it was made: so would run the Christian account. And we share this Creation's particular sort of solidity. Our flesh and bones and viscera are at home in this blueness and wetness and sweetness. And all of these "-nesses" present themselves to us in blueberries, and in the water of Lake Maggiore, and in the feathers of the indigo bunting, or in the color of my true love's eyes. I, unlike the archangel Raphael, do not live amongst blue-ness: I live under a blue sky and wear a pullover knitted with blue yarn. It is the kind of creature I am.

Myth is the sort of narrative par excellence which bespeaks most nearly my being this kind of creature. It addresses at the profoundest level the unity which binds us mortals into the integrity of body and soul which we mean when we say "man" or "woman." To speak to us as though we are a sort of paste-up job of nonmaterial and material substances is to do us a sad disservice. That toe they just had to amputate was *me*, somehow: *I* am lessened by the surgery. It is I who ache with this migraine. My stomach is wrenched and my tear ducts overflow over this grief that has come upon me. My muscles tighten and my forehead sweats and my adrenalin rushes when danger approaches. In all of our experience, there is very little separating out of the components that make us what we are, namely, body and soul. In death we are tragically disfranchised and sundered, and our souls yearn for the Resurrection, presumably, since we were not made to be nonmaterial. The Resurrection—that flagrantly and embarrassingly physical event—is the great triumph over all Gnosticism.

And myth is the kind of narrative that approaches most nearly the kind of integrity which we believe about the Resurrection, or, more to our purpose here, about the Incarnation. In the Incarnation you have the seamless integrity of form and content. The Incarnation is not a symbol. Nor is it even a metaphor. It is That Towards Which all symbol and metaphor strain. For in symbol and metaphor, and in all of art, you have the effort to make B stand for A, or B suggest A, or B evoke A, or B make A present. The octagonal signpost at the corner of the two streets means stop. The shamrock means Ireland. The gold ring means married. The trumpets mean Here comes the king.

When you raise this to the level of art, we find ourselves drawn into a subterfuge that seems to bespeak matters of vast weight. We will all cooperate with Rembrandt in allowing oily pigments spread over canvas to "be" Aristotle Contemplating the Bust of Homer. We will be accomplices with van Eyck in agreeing that that flat surface with the tints on it "is" the Mystic Lamb of St. John's Apocalypse.

In all of these situations you have B (a shape; a color; oil paint) standing in for A. And it is thus with all of the arts, which are in some sense activities which touch exquisitely on the sort of creature we mortals are, since they seem to spring from the deepest levels of our being, and to reach to our origins. Certainly art is proto-historic, ubiquitous, and unremitting. You cannot stop us painting, dancing, singing, and telling stories.

Telling stories. Another activity that is protohistoric, ubiquitous, and unremitting, and seems to touch on the central mystery of our humanity. In drama, we do all sorts of pretending. We allow the amphitheater to be Thebes, or the Globe to be Verona, and we allow John Gielgud to be Hamlet or Paul Scofield to be Lear. And not only that. By a sort of alchemy, we are pleased to see Hamlet or Lear to be us. That is, when Hamlet mutters his tortured ratiocinations, we thrill at hearing our own deepest perplexities given perfect shape. Lear is a frightening warning to us not to allow ourselves vanity and foolishness like that. His grandeur is our grandeur, and his peril our peril. In all of this it is the fiction that, paradoxically, bundles us, not away from what is serious, but towards it.

Myth is the kind of narrative that most nearly approaches this same seamlessness of form and content which our own personhood manifests. For there is no "meaning" in myth to be precipitated out like curds. Theseus's labyrinth does not "mean" complexity, for example: it is a labyrinth. Hercules does not "mean" prowess: he is a big strong hero. The Gardens of the Hesperides do not mean the fulfillment of desire: they are ultimate gardens. In this sense myth defies interpretation, since when we interpret we winnow out of the

stuff something else, namely, meaning. We do this win-
nowing most characteristically with Shakespeare's plays,
say, and with all narratives in some sense, of course.
Henry James and James Joyce positively cry out for this
treatment. But with the myths, insofar as we put a
Jungian or Freudian, or even "literary" interpretation on
them, we feel that we have in some sense put them in
a Procrustean bed. Or, to change the metaphor, we have
driven a wedge between form and content. In order to
do justice to the fabric we have to leave it as it is. We
have to connive wholeheartedly in the fiction if we want
to have the full worth of it.

If this seems too precious, we may recall the obvious
here: when we mortals make our supreme attempt to
raid the precincts of reality, we indulge in fictions. We
play let's pretend. For in the deepest, most serious experiences which attend our mortality, namely, birth, marriage, and death, we sense that we are in precincts that
resist the efforts of proposition and statement to penetrate them. So, by way, not of escaping the full force of
the experiences, but rather of entering more deeply into
them, we play. We pretend. When the obstetricians and
clipboards and midwifery have done all they can do vis-
à-vis birth, we bring out the candles and the champagne,
neither of which does the slightest bit of good on the
utilitarian front. Marriage: when we have signed the li-
cense and have made our solemn pledges to each other
privately, then again we "play": elaborate costume, pro-
cession, public ceremony, highly wrought ritual—this is
all an effort to vouchsafe the truth to us, not to escape
from it. Nay, we know that the play—the ritual or the
ceremony—is the only method available to our humanity
by which we may enter fully into the meaning. And
death: long palls, drawn hearses, nodding plumes, crepe,
winding sheets, hatchments: none of it is worth a
ha'penny on the rational front. But we have outstripped
the solely rational and its resources in these precincts.

Ceremony and art and fiction, and most notably myth, turn out upon reflection to be indispensable. But that is too weak a word. Those phenomena bear in their very texture the texture of reality. The propositional, the discursive, the ratiocinative, the abstract—these, too, bespeak reality after their own species, and to the utmost of their powers. But if we wish to descry Reality, then we are going to be aware that from the fountainhead of Reality we find rumbling at us, not just decrees from Sinai, and not only books from the prophets, but also stars and sun and moon and earth and water and rock and strawberries and the bodies of man and woman. And we will be aware of the fact that the redeeming of all of this, when it had fallen into ruin, came at us in the pelts of animals slain by the Lord God to cover our nakedness, and in the stone of altars and the blood and burned fat of goats and lambs, and in hyssop and incense and gold and purple. And in the culmination of that drama we find, not the transcending of all that Hebrew tackle and gear, but, lo, a conceiving and a gestation and a parturition and suckling; and water to wine at a wedding; and stones made bread; and a fast in the wilderness; and, finally, our salvation played out with whips and thorns and nails, and then a body out of the grave and taken into the midmost mystery of the Holy Trinity. All very solid.

Christians see in that story not mere surface events with a subsurface meaning that can be teased out of it all. The events *are* the meaning. The Incarnation *is* the Eternal Word at its most characteristic. Islam has a book; so far they are like us in that we also have a book. But unlike Islam, Christianity celebrates an Incarnation: the ineffable becomes solid with the particular solidity that belongs to this Creation in which we belong.

The myths are the stories par excellence which never let us dissociate ourselves for one instant from the solid. We cannot fend off the texture of the myths with a cerebral or propositional barge pole. We have to stay with Ulysses as he dodges Polyphemus's boulders, and with his men as they grunt and snuffle, having been turned into pigs by Circe, and with Leda as the swan ravishes her. Humiliating as it may be to our sense of our own cerebral dignity, we find that we live in a story like that.

We live in a story in which the Lord God is to be found walking in the garden in the cool of the day. We live in a story in which men build a great tower with a top aimed at heaven. We live in a story in which a great boat saves the remnant of animals and men, and a bush burns with the presence of the deity whose name is I AM, and a great horn blows so loudly from the mountain that the people cry out to Moses to intercede for them, and the King of Heaven is found in a stall, and the whole of mankind is redeemed by the torture endured in the flesh of one man, and the dead rise. It is a mythic narrative, surely?

Yes, but with this slight difference. Christians believe that in this last set of events, that which all the other myths strained towards, the god made himself known to us, actually stepped through the scrim that hangs between the seen and the unseen, out into the light of real, historical, geographical day. Myth became Fact.

And the events in this enormous drama are such that we find that sheer proposition will not quite do the trick, much as our rational selves would be gratified to discover that it would. And we also find that in the presence of these events, we mortals must do what we always do with the ineffable: we must enter into them by means of ceremony. We must eat actual bread and drink real wine, and go down into real water. Our whole flesh cries out to be allowed to do obeisance, and to hear the organ and sweet voices, and to smell the incense. Our piety yearns to fasten upon the Story, since it is a true story on the one hand, and, on the other hand, since the truth can only be got at, finally, by means of story.

Author Biography

Thomas Howard is professor of English at St. John's Seminary in Boston. He is married and has two grown children. He holds degrees from Wheaton College, the University of Illinois, and New York University. His books currently in print include *On Being Catholic, If Your Mind Wanders at Mass, C. S. Lewis: Man of Letters, Evangelical Is Not Enough, Chance or the Dance,* and *Lead, Kindly Light.*

During my years as chair of English at Wheaton College, I frequently invited Madeleine L'Engle to speak at conferences on Christianity and literature, to give special lectures, and to teach creative writing for brief sessions. It was a special privilege to be in her presence. She meant more to me personally than one can translate into sentences. Other members of the Department of English joined me in deep appreciation for the way in which she championed and educated the imagination with her special communicative warmth and conviction.

None of us, including generations of students, can ever forget her telling us of her approach to writing: "I try to serve my work, to listen to it, and to go where the work wants me to go." How many times did she kindly remind us that a work of art is creative; it is a way of naming a thing, an experience, an action, and a person in order to bring it into a new and effectual existence.

Thank you, Madeleine, for yourself, for your unusual kind of gentleness, tolerance, and generosity. Thank you for being a friend.

E. Beatrice Batson

8
The Incarnation and Poets-Priests: Herbert and Hopkins

E. Beatrice Batson

When Shakespeare's Prince Hamlet considers a potential plan to uncover the possible crime of the reigning king in order to satisfy his longing to know the truth about a suspicious act of murder, he turns to drama or to what he later calls "a miraculous organ." An inherent characteristic of art—or this miraculous organ—is the power to bring about in an indirect manner a new discernment and fuller understanding by framing and depicting the known in an unfamiliar context or in an unusual manner.

Prince Hamlet is not alone in his grasp for the meaning and understanding of reality. What each of us earnestly desires is to gain access to a resource or storehouse which embodies things as they really are and at the same time to discover a way that yields far more than one-dimensional, discursive language is able to unfold. In our lack of satisfaction with the fact alone or the thing itself we enjoy a great company of writers and thinkers, including Plato, Augustine, Aquinas, Martin

Luther, John Calvin, not to mention Moses, the prophets, the apostle Paul, and Jesus himself. Having made this claim, we must underscore that such a position neither denies nor ignores FACTS, and certainly not the temporal. We turn to imagistic or metaphorical language, or indeed to art, to direct us in our quest for insights that stretch beyond the yieldings of expository language.

In her book *Speaking in Parables* Sallie McFague writes of metaphorical language as a "mirror of our constitution: the unity of body and soul, outer and inner, familiar and unfamiliar, known and unknown." She further holds that metaphorical language "makes connections, sees resemblances, uniting body and soul—earthly, temporal, ordinary experience with its meaning."[1] In brief, this is the essence of art: taking the ordinary, familiar experience and giving it a new order, shape and form. What McFague states is true of the verbal arts and of all art.

What we should also emphasize is that the Christian faith frequently becomes an informing body of belief for numerous writers who are Christian. To conclude this is only to think on the writings of Dante, Spenser, Shakespeare (his writings certainly have a Christian dimension), Donne, Herbert, Crashaw, Milton, Browning, Longfellow, Dostoevski, and, more recently, Greene, Eliot (T. S.), Solzhenitsyn, and others, including the beloved contemporary writer Madeleine L'Engle. What is also obvious is that these writers often show a desire to explore the relationship between their faith and their art. Few authors, however, feel the compulsion to justify in detail the way faith informs writing as does John Bunyan, the seventeenth-century allegorist and Dissenter. Before his well-known allegory, *The Pilgrim's Progress,* actually begins, Bunyan undoubtedly deems it necessary to write a rhymed preface, defending the form his work takes. Whether he believes that he must justify his mode to those critics who may expect only expository, discursive writing from a Dissenter who frequently wrote exhortatory prose, or whether he simply wishes to show that there is a mysterious relationship between what God became in the Incarnation and what an artist does in his created work is difficult to determine. Without question there is an obvious tension in Bunyan's aesthetic between the didactic mode and the imaginative method of literary writing. Regardless of explanations for his writing it, no one can think of his rhymed preface as a jumble of jejune words, for in it Bunyan manages to sharpen some of the major principles which concern the Christian and art. It is not my desire or purpose, however, to focus on Bunyan or on his reasons for writing a preface to his famous allegory, published in 1678, which became an immediate success and was for many years the book, next to the Bible, most deeply cherished in the English-speaking world. I do wish to show that Bunyan offers considerable wisdom on the relation between art and the Incarnation and underscores important features which outstanding artists embody in their imaginative works. To show the latter, we will look at a few poems written by two poets whose poetry clearly reveals the glory and the mystery of art as incarnation.

If we wish, then, to see the facets of Bunyan's thinking on imaginative writing and to discover principles which he believes to be essential to fictional creations, it is necessary to look briefly at parts of his rhymed preface to *The Pilgrim's Progress*.

A major thrust of the preface is his persuasion that art is no enemy of truth. To give support to this important principle, Bunyan summons the authority of the Bible and writes:

The prophets used much by metaphors
To set forth truth; yea, who so considers
Christ, his apostles too, shall plainly see
That truths to this day in such mantles be.[2]

Not only does he hold that he has the highest authority for writing metaphorically, but he also asserts that there is no stronger way to unfold truth than through metaphorical language. For Bunyan, there is unquestionably great merit in *showing* a man on his journey from this world to the next—as he does in his famous allegory—instead of always *telling, instructing,* and *exhorting* him as to exactly how he should make the journey.

Bunyan knows well the stories and parables in the Bible; he sees too that familiar and commonplace words such as seeds, bread, camels, birds, sheep, swine, and other ordinary words may become suggestive of a truth and a reality beyond themselves. He argues that "base things usher in Divine" and to unite the ordinary and commonplace with the mysterious and transcendent is the way of metaphor. In brief, it is one way of viewing art as incarnation.

Furthermore, Bunyan clearly suggests that what he is attempting to do in his allegory has a relationship to what God becomes in the Incarnation. To state that relationship in the following manner undoubtedly comes close to what Bunyan holds: as the Incarnate God, the Word, is the physical embodiment of the Divine and transcendent, so the written word is capable of showing the profoundly transcendent through the familiar, the known, and the ordinary. As a writer, Bunyan believes that he must incarnate the spiritual in terms of the immediate, the literal, and the commonplace. What he definitely holds is that truth in "swaddling clouts" (swaddling clothes—undoubtedly he refers to Luke 2:12):

Informs the judgement, rectifies the mind,
Pleases the understanding, makes the will
Submit; the memory too, it doth fill
With what doth our imagination please.[3]

Whether or not Bunyan's own use of "figures and similitudes" in his dream allegory always nourishes an imagination starved for truth in metaphorical language is, in some minds, subject to debate, but he well understands that the mysteries of art bear a relationship to the unparalleled mystery of God becoming flesh. He also knows that metaphorical language has the distinctive quality of setting the familiar in a new context that causes words to mean more than they ordinarily do and thereby reveals new meanings and fresh insights.

Readers will recall how he fills his imagined story with visualizations of the world he knows best—the rural world of Bedford, England, and its environs. Somehow those ordinary terms such as muddy roads, ragged clothes, a miry slough, disagreeable weather, a barking dog, dark villages, and steep hills may suggest more than a mere reflection of his realistic world. He desires a language that unfolds a perception of reality that shows transcendent truth and, at the same time, "penetrates the judgment, the mind, the will" of each finite human being. The fact that he writes at length to justify the non-expository form his work takes reveals the depth of Bunyan's commitment to "similitudes." As does any artist, he seeks to make real the spiritual in temporal and physical terms.

Regardless of what one may think of the relationship between what he writes in the rhymed preface and what he does in his allegory, it is fair to state, I believe, that Bunyan writes theory that points up important features of art, including metaphorical or symbolical language and art as incarnation. While other artists who are Christians focus on the relationship between their art and their faith perhaps in less minute detail than he, all give thought to the metaphor, the symbol, and the form which unfold their vision. Each one seeks to incarnate God and to make real the transcendent in temporal terms. In Book V of Milton's *Paradise Lost*, Raphael apparently speaks for Milton as artist in these words:

how shall I relate
To human sense th' invisible exploits
Of warring Spirits . . .
how last unfold
The secrets of another world, perhaps
Not lawful to reveal? Yet for thy good
This is dispens't, and what surmounts the reach
Of human sense I shall delineate so,
By likening spiritual to corporal forms,
As may express them best. . . .[4]

What Milton suggests through Raphael, and what Bunyan points up in the rhymed preface, are concerns for
those artists who are Christians to show through metaphor—and through an incarnational act—how Christian
belief informs their art. Two poets, one from the seventeenth century and one from the nineteenth, may help
readers understand more fully the glory of metaphor
and the beauty and power of art as incarnation in poetry.

The poet-priest of Bemerton, England, George Herbert of the seventeenth century, writes a body of poems
which poetically argue his indebtedness to the Bible.
Almost every aspect of his poetry particularly demon-
strates the influence of wisdom literature, the Psalms,
the parables of Christ, and Pauline writings. To see these
influences is not to deny that Herbert conceives of poetry in Richard Hughes's terms as "a miniature version
of the Incarnation."[5] While Herbert rarely uses the actual
term *incarnation*, there is no question regarding his
beliefs and feelings about the ramifications of this important Christian doctrine. Perhaps it is helpful or interesting to know, however, that although the Incarnation
embraces the birth, the ministry, and the death of Christ,
Herbert gives greatest emphasis to the passion and
death of Christ. Obviously for Herbert, the passion and
death is the central activity of the redemptive process.[6]

This poet does not ignore the nativity or the life and

ministry of Christ; at the same time, his poetry suggests that the Incarnation never fails to provide him with subject or form and meaning. In a poem with a subject which he rarely uses, I should like to study Herbert's poetry as incarnation. In his poem "Christmas" he writes of a strayed rider who arrives at an inn where the Host not only receives him, but waits for any traveler in need of help. The poet soon evokes the Nativity scene, which embodies one who "Wrapt' in night's mantle, stole into a manger." What one perceives is one strayed rider who becomes a metaphor for all strayed riders. It is of special interest that when the strayed rider alludes to the Nativity, he does so across the "distance of the centuries," with the cross and the tomb—indeed the whole Christian story—ingrained on his mind, and as ingrained as the manger in the inn.

To read even a few poems by Herbert is to recognize that the Christian doctrine of the Incarnation cannot be limited to the small number of his poems whose explicit subject is the Incarnation itself; rather, his sense of the Incarnation, its embodiment of the entire Christian story, pervades his poetry, and each poem that he writes is a celebration of the Incarnation. It is equally clear that Herbert's "heaven in ordinaire"—an important phrase from his poem "Prayer"—comes very close to a formulation of the poet's view of metaphorical language and a fuller view of the way he envisions the implications of the Incarnation. This means language that never takes one out of everyday reality but drives a reader more deeply into reality. When he selects ordinary words like church floor, a collar, a flower, a pulley, a lute, a wreath, a piece of wood, bread and water, birds, sheep and fish, and doors and keys, Herbert makes no attempt to deny the usual settings and meanings of the words; rather, in them he offers opportunity in his incarnational act to probe new meanings and insights beyond the ordinary. As Bunyan argues for Christ's use of metaphor, so also

C. A. Patrides contends that the "Biblical burden of Herbert's . . . images is manifest in the light of Christ's habitual resort to the familiar things of daily life. . . ." In Herbert, accordingly, there are clusters of images: one group derives from its natural order, one from commercial and legal activities, and one from architecture. In fact, architectural imagery is the central image of several of Herbert's poems, including the two well-known poems "The World" and "Man."[7]

Although it is not possible now to study the language of every poem, I should like to examine another poem which focuses on a traveler who comes to an inn. In this last poem by Herbert, and in his poem "Christmas," there is no specific reference to the Nativity scene. In this poem, he celebrates, I believe, incarnate love or divine love. Even though some readers see the poem as a dramatic depiction of the Protestant belief in justification by faith (a reading worthy of strong support), this last poem of *The Temple* is another "miniature version of the Incarnation." Consider this beautiful poem, "Love III":

Love bade me welcome; Yet my soul drew back,
Guilty of dust and sin.
But quick-ey'd Love, observing me grow slack
From my first entrance in,
Drew nearer to me, sweetly questioning,
If I lacked any thing.

A guest, I answer'd, worthy to be here:
Love said, You shall be he.
I the unkinde, ungratefull? Ah my deare,
I cannot look on thee.
Love took my hand, and smiling did reply,
Who made the eyes but I?

Truth Lord, but I have marr'd them: let my shame
Go where it doth deserve.

And know you not, sayes Love, who bore the blame?
My deare, then I will serve.
You must sit down, sayes Love, and taste my meat:
So I did sit and eat.[8]

The temporal figure of an untidy traveler arriving at an inn welcomed by a gracious host is the framework of the poem. What appears in the first stanza to be hardly more than a social situation, with a dusty traveler hesitant to accept the hospitality of the host, soon takes on a profoundly transcendent meaning. The gracious attitude and kind actions of the host are touching from the beginning.

In the first stanza, the host bids the traveler "welcome," later observes the reluctance of the guest, then draws nearer and "sweetly" questions whether he "lacked any thing." The guest's reply to the question is terse: "A guest, I answered, worthy to be here." Even more abrupt is the host's response: "You shall be he." Combined with his reluctant, self-conscious spirit, the guest shows a strong unwillingness to accept the view of the host as depicted in the dialogue of almost all of the second stanza.

To remember that one is reading George Herbert, especially at this point in the poem, is helpful, for he will not allow any travel-worn "guest" to win the unfolding debate. Love, transcendent Love, warmly extends an invitation to all who "are guilty of sin and shame" to accept a gift, a gift completely unmerited.

Among the many suggestions of this powerfully metaphorical poem is that feelings of worthiness or unworthiness must give way to the serious act of "sitting down" and "tasting." As the poem closes, the familiar figure of a begrimed traveler vividly remains in a reader's mind and imagination, but also compelling is the glorious understanding that through the language of metaphor, influenced by his belief in the historical act of the

Incarnation, Herbert certainly takes us not out of reality, but he drives any reader more deeply into it.

If he finds in the truth of the Incarnation both doctrinal and artistic purposes, Herbert knows why this is so and why this leads him to write as he does. Before looking at any length at another of his poems, it is perhaps wise to look briefly at some of his own suggestions on his language.

When he writes that he envies "no man's nightingale or spring" and requests that others not punish him "with loss of rime / who plainly says my God, my King," Herbert is by no means offering a protest against poets who choose subjects and language different from his. He does not believe, however, that poets differing from him have a monopoly on poetry. Without question, a poem such as "Jordan I" shows that God's love and love for God are appropriate subjects for poetry. In a sonnet to his mother, he earnestly questions why poets do not write of God's love and offer burnt offerings of lays upon his altar, and he sincerely ponders whether God's Dove cannot outstrip that of Cupid. For Herbert, there is no question as to which is the more significant.

In "Jordan II," when he hears the whisper of a friend: "There is in love a sweetness readie penned / Copie out only that and save expense," Herbert does not suggest that writers forsake the rigorous pondering, keen sensibility, and the frequent aloneness of the poet. He does see that the "sweetness" of Christ "ready-penned" is available to writers in the richly metaphorical beauty of the created world, and that each writer searches for the appropriate language to depict that "sweetness." What concerns Herbert in "Jordan II" is the way in which in his earlier poems, he attempts to "deck" and "clothe" in "quaint words" and to "weave" himself "into the sense," but the concerns and anxieties appear to cease with "the whisper" of a friend. When he speaks about "copying out" the sweetness "ready penned," Herbert refers to that sweetness "revealed in God's manifested love (that is, in Christ.") To copy out that sweetness refers to more than finding a literary style; to paraphrase Rosemond Tuve, it entails showing in his poems manifestations of Christ's love and demonstrations of the Spirit.[9] In Ellen Rickey's thinking, moreover, "verbal plainness" for Herbert has to do with sharpness of expression, and its antithesis is not beauty but "pretension and imagerial clutter"[10] Although he refuses to state or suggest that plain and simple language may lead to profound insights, it is equally true that Herbert cannot fully accept the thought that plainness of style is to be equated with creative or intellectual poverty.

It is the metaphor of music that sustains the poetry of a favorite poem of mine. What the poem does is to celebrate the Crucifixion and the Resurrection. In "Easter," Herbert addresses his musical instrument, the lute, to celebrate the two great events, and he depicts the Christ as perfect harmony:

> *Awake, my lute, and struggle for thy part*
>   *With all thy art.*
> *The cross taught all wood to resound his name,*
>   *Who bore the same.*
> *His stretched sinews taught all strings, what key*
> *Is best to celebrate this most high day.*[11]

Since Christ's death on a wooden cross invests wood with new significance, the "cross" of the third line becomes a pattern for all wood. Herbert's art is metaphorically in debt to the passion of Christ; wood provides the form of Christ's crucifixion, but at the same time, wood shaped into a musical instrument offers praise to the resurrected Lord in resounding his name.

What is at once striking is the close parallel between the fifth and third lines: As the "cross taught all wood," so the "stretched sinews," says Herbert, "taught all strings." I remember with pleasure one of my former students clearly reminding readers that "taught" is a pun on "taut," and that metaphorical implications are quite startling in Herbert's juxtaposition of "wood" and "strings" with "stretched sinews" and the "cross." The grandeur at this point is the vividness with which a lute incarnates the crucified Christ, and the lute strings vividly depict the flesh of the Christ stretched across the wood of the cross. Those "stretched sinews" taught all strings "what key is best to celebrate this high day."

In his celebration of the crucified, risen Christ, Herbert turns to the "Original harmony" to find the right key. Once again, this poet-priest, George Herbert, shows the capacity of the physical in poetic hands to embody the transcendent. He finds the Original of all metaphors in the sacrifice of the Incarnate Son, and upon this sacred pattern Herbert shapes his celebration and praise.

If the Incarnation provides theological and artistic foundations for the seventeenth-century poet-priest, so also is this Christian doctrine equally significant for the nineteenth-century poet-priest Gerard Manley Hopkins. Writing poetry informed by the Christian faith at the end of an era powerfully influenced by materialism may seem an unlikely enterprise to undertake. Hopkins does exactly this! In distinctive ways, he might also be called a modern poet, particularly in his ability to show the power of concrete things to depict states of the mind and of the inner self. Few readers of Hopkins can easily forget his supreme power in equating high mountains with the frustration and desolation of the mind. Ponder again these words:

*O the mind, mind has mountains; cliffs of fall
Frightful, sheer, no-man-fathomed. Hold them cheap
May who ne'er hung there.*[12]

If he looks inward, Hopkins also turns outward and upward and sees God's signature in the glory of creation. See his discoveries: "The world is charged with the grandeur of God" or "Look at the stars! look, look up at the skies / O look at all the fire-folk sitting in the air!" and "Glory be to God for dappled things." Throughout his poetry, there is a metaphorical declaration that the central fact of all the world is the Incarnation. Paul Mariani says of Hopkins's poetry that "the Incarnation is operative in time and space, in Hopkins's time as in Christ's, in Wales as in Galilee . . . there is news of God everywhere for those who are properly receptive."[13] All nature is sacramental in that it is a visible sign of an intelligent Creator at work in a world centered in the Incarnate Christ.

Perhaps it is of value to mention that Hopkins shows a concern over the way careless human beings are prone to mar the beauty of an ordered creation and bring about an apparent fragmentation. If readers recall "God's Grandeur," they remember that at the beginning of the poem, the emphasis is on the grandeur of God, manifest in at least two ways: at times this grandeur "will flame out, like shining from shook foil," but over a period of time, it "gathers to a greatness, like the ooze of oil." The poet stops on this latter or second way, and the word "crushed" begins the fourth line of the poem, and he reveals why he uses "crushed":

Generations have trod, have trod, have trod;
   And all is seared with trade; bleared, smeared
      with toil;
   And wears man's smudge and shares man's smell:
      the soil
Is bare now, nor can foot feel, being shod.[14]

Hopkins's reference to the "crushing" of the created world is not a mere commentary on the environment, but what human beings do to the earth and world un-

doubtedly troubles him. Although this great metaphorical writer clearly sees the ugly concrete details of a
"seared," "bleared," and "smeared" temporal world with
its smudges and smells, his vision embodies a greater
reality. His poetry is redemptive, bringing order out of
brokenness and beauty out of ugliness. Readers should
also hear:

And for all this, nature is never spent;
There lives the dearest freshness deep down things;
And though the last lights off the black West went
Oh, morning, at the brown brink eastward, springs—
Because the Holy Ghost over the bent
World broods with warm breast and with ah! bright
wings. [15]

Once more, Hopkins allows the various parts of the poetic whole to work together to incarnate the extraordinary: the source of the ever-renewed life in creation is
God and his great love manifest in the Holy Ghost. To
see even glimpses of his radical metaphors and dense
images is to discover that Hopkins is a celebrator.

In "The Windhover," a poem which he calls the best
thing he ever wrote, the poet celebrates the beauty and
splendor of Christ, particularly in his sacrificial suffering.
To unfold what some call his "radical particularity," Hopkins juxtaposes a plethora of metaphors. The first few
lines show the incredibly majestic flight of the windhover in terms of a vision in early morning: "I caught
this morning morning's minion, king- / dom of daylight's
dauphin, dapple-dawn-drawn Falcon, in his riding / the
rolling level underneath him steady air, and striding /
High there, how he rung upon the rein of a wimpling
wing / In his ecstasy!"[16] The grace and nobility of the
natural beauty of the Falcon is, however, only a small
flash of that splendor whose power, beauty, and nobility
belong to another realm and order.

Pondering those first few lines of the poem, Donald McChesney concludes that it is not that he merely finds "an analogy for spiritual beauty in the material world," but that Hopkins "is pointing to the hidden and terrible splendor of sacrificial suffering which breaks forth upon the world when all is accomplished."[17] Recall that the spiraling, gliding bird suddenly buckles, but see and hear Hopkins:

> *Brute beauty and valour and act, oh, air, pride,*
>   *plume, here*
> *Buckle! And the fire that breaks from thee then, a*
>   *billion*
> *Times told lovelier, more dangerous, O my chevalier!*
> *No wonder of it: shéer plód makes plough down*
>   *sillion*
> *Shine, and blue-beak embers, ah my dear,*
> *Fall, gall themselves, and gash gold-vermilion.*[18]

If readers look long at the images of buckling, gashing, galling—indeed all images—of the poem which recall the sacrificial suffering and see the climax, "gash gold-vermilion" not merely as heraldic colors but as the royal blood from Christ's wounds or his gashings, then McChesney's observation is strikingly perceptive. His view is similar to Sallie McFague's conclusion that obviously something beautiful and shining comes out of natural things, but for her, the poem is a "parable of the crucifixion," and she adds that "there is no way of exhausting the significance of the poem's possibility of helping us encounter the crucifixion. . . ."[19] In showing the particularity of the bird's flight and death, Hopkins places one complex image on the other to create not only a vision of a beautiful, majestic bird in flight but also a vivid picture of transcendent truth.

Numerous poems by Hopkins, including many not noted here, reach ecstatic heights. This undoubtedly springs from his belief that the undercurrent of creative energy that supports and binds together the created world, giving things shape, form, and meaning, embodies the energy of God himself. Precisely, the outward and visible beauty is to Hopkins the reflection of the energy, invisible glory, and beauty of the Creator God. His highly charged metaphorical language is a normal result of his equally highly charged convictions. His poetic world is a dynamic world; all is moving, urgent, and energetic. Yet, in his bold language, which at times also shows an almost unequaled compression, Hopkins makes contact with a Supreme God, a God who can be rejected, wrestled with, surrendered to, worshiped, and found in the most familiar places. This eternal Being is so powerful and glorious that one may stand before him in almost unbearable awe, but this glorious Being is never far removed from human beings. To remind us of his nearness, think only of those lovely lines from Hopkins's memorable "The Wreck of the Deutschland": "his going in Galilee; / Warm-laid grave of a womb-life grey; / Manger, maiden's knee; / The dense and the driven Passion, and frightful sweat."[20]

Even though one may frequently see Hopkins's radical metaphors, his urgency of emotional experience, and the organic function of his imagery, one must not overlook an equally important feature of his poetry: the simple or childlike images like thrush's eggs, poor sheep's back, a swooping hawk, dappled cows, matchwood, fallen chestnuts, crushed olives, and perhaps not simple but memorable "immortal diamond." In the realism of the simpler images, Hopkins resembles Herbert and like Herbert recognizes in these simple creatures a doctrinal and artistic purpose.

George Herbert and Gerard M. Hopkins, poets and priests, share a view of metaphor informed by a belief in the truth of the Incarnation. Both are poets who are at the same time Christians, but neither represses his apprehension of this world in writing of the transcendent. Both poets draw upon materials from the natural world, from tradition, and from experience. With painstakingly disciplined art, both order these materials into gems of beauty, unfolding truth. Both are celebrators; Hopkins with his radical metaphor and density of images and Herbert with his simple (never simplistic) language and "homely images" celebrate the Incarnation. Both show a world in its infinite variety as one coherent and centered in the Incarnate Christ. Both unquestionably demonstrate what Bunyan struggled to uncover: there is a relationship between the mysteries of art and the unparalleled mystery of God becoming flesh. Both Herbert and Hopkins leave us awe-struck as we behold a "miraculous organ" in their celebration of art as Incarnation.

Author Biography

E. Beatrice Batson, Ph.D., a member of the English faculty at Wheaton College in Wheaton, Illinois, for thirty years (twelve years as chair), is now coordinator of Wheaton's Shakespeare Special Collection, which focuses on the Christian dimension of Shakespeare's writings. She is the author of several books, including *Allegory and the Imagination*, many chapters for books edited by scholars, and numerous journal articles and book reviews. She is also a frequent lecturer on college and university campuses throughout the United States and Canada.

I first met Madeleine in 1974 at the Green Lake Writers' Conference where we were part of the small, congenial faculty gathered by director Mel Lorentzen. Mel was master of the revels and each evening led us in punning, singing, charades, and other parlor games. Madeleine introduced us to the games "dictionary" and "adverb." In the latter, one player performs an action in the manner of an adverb until another guesses what the adverb is. I recall the hilarity that greeted Madeleine when, assuming a severely decorous look, she tickled the piano keys with one foot to illustrate the adverb *sensuously.*

I had published a book of poems the year before and was venturing for the first time to write fantasy. I'd brought along a story for Madeleine to read. She not only read it but gave me warm encouragement, saying, "This is a fairy tale, and it is meant for *adults.*" When *Alpha Centauri* and *Whalesong* appeared, she welcomed them with praise more generous than a writer dare hope for, even from a friend. For her generous enthusiasm and support as well as for the hilarity and fellowship of Green Lake I shall always be grateful.

Robert Siegel

9
A World of Light: "The Retreate," by Henry Vaughan

Robert Siegel

I didn't hear the last lines because my mind stopped with A deep but dazzling darkness. *And then it picked up the poem he'd read, with eternity being* a great ring of pure and endless light.
—Madeleine L'Engle, *A Ring of Endless Light*

There are poems all of us who love poetry return to in order to rediscover our first love of poetry—those moments of revelation or ecstasy that originally drew us under its spell. Or at least I suspect it is true of all, for I know it is true of myself and venture it is so of the author of the above passage. Such poems, or lines and passages from them, become places where the soul rests and feeds, or a "fountain-light of all our day"—to steal a metaphor from Wordsworth.

For many, as for the friend and author we celebrate here, among these poems are a handful of lyrics by Henry Vaughan, the seventeenth-century physician and Christian Neo-Platonist, whose concern with what he called the world of light, as opposed to the shadow-world of ordinary existence, occupies most of his poetry:

"The Retreate"

Happy those early dayes! when I
Shin'd in my Angell-infancy.
Before I understood this place
Appointed for my second race,
Or taught my soul to fancy aught
But a white, Celestiall thought,
When yet I had not walk'd above
A mile or two from my first Love,
And looking back (at that short space.)
Could see a glimpse of his bright face;
When on some gilded Cloud, or flowre
My gazing soul would dwell an houre,
And in those weaker glories spy
Some shadows of eternity.
Before I taught my tongue to wound
My Conscience with a sinfull sound,
Or had the black art to dispence
A sev'rall sinne to ev'ry sence.
But felt through all this fleshly dresse
Bright shootes of everlastingnesse.
  O how I long to travel back
And tread again that ancient track!
That I might once more reach that plaine
Where first I left my glorious traine.
From whence th'Inlightned spirit sees
That shady City of Palme trees;
But (ah!) my soul with too much stay
Is drunk, and staggers in the way.
Some men a forward motion love,
But I by backward steps would move,
And when this dust falls to the urn
In that state I came return.

What chiefly sticks in the mind from Vaughan's poems
are the recurring images of light (and darkness), such

as these from "The Retreate,"

Happy those early days! when I
Shin'd in my Angell-infancy.
. . . .
Or taught my soul to fancy aught
But a white, Celestiall thought,
. . . .
But felt through all this fleshly dresse
Bright shootes of everlastingnesse,

and these from other of his poems:

I saw Eternity the other night,
Like a great Ring of pure and endless light,
All calm, as it was bright.

—"The World"

They are all gone into the world of light.

—"Untitled"

There is in God (some say)
A deep but dazzling darkness,

—"The Night"

There is a clarity, simplicity, and power to these images of light that is found in few other poets.

Like Milton's or Blake's, Vaughan's Christian Neo-Platonism is central to his poetry. One may not agree with it and still appreciate his artistry, but one cannot ignore it, for it is at the heart of his poems. Vaughan explains the title of his book, *Silex Scintillans,* in these words: "Certaine Divine Raies breake out of the Soul in adversity, like sparks of fire out of the afflicted flint." He suffered a number of losses at the time of writing these poems, including the death of a beloved brother and the failure of the Royalist cause, and wrote out of his grief. Reading him, one feels that, like his contemporary George Herbert, he brings "authentic tidings of invisible things."

Expressing what Aldous Huxley has called the "perennial philosophy," Vaughan wrote poems concerned with a reality behind the tapestry of human consciousness. It is partly this 'perennial', Neo-Platonism, which I first encountered in Spenser, that drew me to poetry. The great shining Presences that radiate through the splendor of Spenser's language in *The Faerie Queene* and elsewhere haunted me, and wherever this underground river surfaced among English or American poets, I was fascinated—especially by the Romantics from Blake to Keats, but also by Hopkins, Whitman, Eliot, and Roethke—not to mention wistful skeptics of the tradition like the Frost of "For Once Then Something." And beyond English and Christianity, I found poets as diverse as Rumi, Baudelaire, and Rilke caught in the same stream. As a college student, I found myself feeding for days on lines like those from "The Retreate." Returning to them after a long while, I still experience their freshness, power, and promise of something beyond language.

The sense that all phenomena reflect some deep, underlying unity, a reality of which we only catch glimpses, and that even the words of a poem are part of the reality that they represent, remains part of many poetic credos. Many would agree with Shelley that the deep truth is imageless, and yet the only way to represent it or allude to it is through images. The images have a profound organic connection to that which they both conceal and reveal.

There are times when reading or writing poetry when I feel the division between the mind and the world fall away, when words rise up as the things they represent and there is a fusion of the perceiver with the perceived. I am convinced that most who love an art may experience something like this; it is perhaps a state similar to that which Plotinus describes in the *Enneads:*

Everything is filled full of life, boiling with life. Things there flow in a way from a single source, not like one particular breath or warmth, but as if there were a single quality containing in itself and preserving all qualities, sweet taste and smell and the quality of wine with all other flavors, visions of colors and all that touch perceives, all too that hearing hears, all tunes and every rhythm.

The quest of the Neo-Platonic poet is at heart religious, both employing and rejecting the images. As St. Augustine claimed, "It is not these that I love when I love my God. And yet, when I love him, it is true that I love a light of a certain kind, a voice, a perfume, an embrace." In other words, "Neither is this Thou, yet this also is Thou."

Poets before Vaughan had used light as a pervasive symbol of transcendent truth. What is new in his poems is the special association of this light with childhood. In "The Retreate" he bemoans the loss of the all-illuminating light he knew in his infancy and childhood. The poem looks forward to the Romantics' exaltation of childhood as a time of spiritual receptivity—especially Blake's *Songs of Innocence* and Wordsworth's "Ode: Intimations of Immortality from Recollections of Early Childhood." In his later treatment of the theme, Wordsworth refers to the Platonic myth of preexistence, and writes, "trailing clouds of glory do we come / From God, who is our home." He addresses the child (any child) as

> *Mighty prophet! seer blest!*
> *On whom those truths do rest,*
> *Which we are toiling all our lives to find,*
> . . . .
> *Thou, over whom thy Immortality*
> *Broods like the Day, a master o'er a slave,*
> *A Presence which is not to be put by.*

According to Plato in the *Republic*, the soul is completely aware of its immortal status before birth but chooses the inevitable forgetfulness that comes with incarnation and growing to adulthood. As Wordsworth describes the process,

Shades of the prison-house begin to close
*   Upon the growing Boy,*
But he beholds the light, and whence it flows.
. . . .
At length the man perceives it die away,
And fade into the light of common day.

The Freudian critique of this view of the child and childhood has long been with us. In essence, according to Freud, those who hold it are mystifying the infant's yearning to return to the womb, to lose the painful sense of separate and individual identity that is the human condition, and to float in a world where he is blissfully unaware of the difference between himself and his surroundings. This desire to abandon the ego—or to see everything as an extension of it (the toddler's prerogative)—is, in short, infantile. Even if it is a wonderful state of mind or feeling, it is foolish for the adult to soberly entertain it.

But Vaughan and Wordsworth might reply that the fact that the physical situation of the infant creates a condition of psychological and spiritual bliss does not rule out the adult experiencing that bliss on a higher level, another turn up the spiral staircase of the individual's development. Indeed, the bliss of existence in the womb and its long after-light may prefigure and prepare for the experience of the mature sage. The Christian mystic who speaks of union with the Godhead, the Buddhist who experiences awakening, or the Hindu who loses the little self in the larger Self or Atman—these often compare their experience to that of the child. One thinks of Jesus' words, "Unless you become as little children . . ." The "white Celestiall thought," then, the expanded consciousness, the cosmic consciousness of a Blake or a Whitman or an ecstatic St. John of the Cross all involve the loss of ego.

Owen Barfield, in his book *Saving the Appearances*, compares the state of the child and the state of the sage. The little child, including perhaps the higher animals and the human race in its infancy, experiences what he calls "original participation"—the sense of profound harmony with the visible universe. The troubling distinctions of later individuation, especially self-consciousness, have not yet arisen. The state of the sage, the seer, the saint, and perhaps the artist (at least when caught up in his art) is, he says, that of "final participation," or "experiencing the presence of God in all things." All the pain of separateness has been experienced, but has been transcended in a sublime identification of the self with the universe (or what lies behind it) and a casting away of the narrow limits of ego.

That Vaughan identifies his mystical yearnings and glimmerings, the sparks flying from the flint of adversity, with the state of the child is therefore not surprising. That he accomplishes this poignantly and economically in sixteen short couplets *is*—and is also what makes this poem live for us three centuries later.

Next to the images of light and the unforgettable phrasing, it is the short couplets themselves that most contribute to the power of the poem. The effect of the couplets here is to mimic the inevitable movement of time. The speaker moves away from the light, as on a walk or in a race:

Happy those early dayes! when I
Shin'd in my Angell-infancy.
Before I understood this place
Appointed for my second race,

Or taught my soul to fancy aught
But a white, Celestiall thought,
When yet I had not walk'd above
A mile or two from my first Love,
And looking back (at that short space.)
Could see a glimpse of his bright face.

The strong meter and the swiftly returning rhyme of the four-beat couplet reinforce the central metaphor of life as movement away from light toward the darkness of adulthood. The effect of time passing quickly here is similar to that of the couplets in Marvell's "To His Coy Mistress":

But at my back I always hear
Time's winged chariot hurrying near.

By Vaughan's fifth couplet, the child is no longer looking directly at the light, but gazing at its diluted glory:

On some gilded Cloud, or flowre
My gazing soul would dwell an houre,
And in those weaker glories spy
Some shadows of eternity.

The developing consciousness and conscience, speech itself, are the source of greater darkness, the "black art" of sinning, in contrast to the earlier state,

Before I taught my tongue to wound
My Conscience with a sinfull sound,
Or had the black art to dispence
A sev'rall sinne to ev'ry sence.

The force of the word "sev'rall" here is to suggest the arrival of duplicity and multiplicity, the loss of unity. ("After one," Lao Tzu said, "there are two; after two, the ten thousand things.")

But the movement reverses itself in the poem's second half, at least in desire:

O how I long to travel back
And tread again that ancient track!
That I might once more reach that plaine
Where first I left my glorious traine.
But (ah!) my soul with too much stay
Is drunk, and staggers in the way.
Some men a forward motion love,
But I by backward steps would move.

The speaker is almost asking for time to reverse itself, or at least to move in two directions at once—as is the case in a Feyn diagram in subatomic physics, where matter moving forward in time and antimatter moving backwards are equally feasible. He would return to his origins, though he admits to having difficulty, is "drunk" and "staggers in the way." Plato had said the soul grows inebriated with life and forgets its divine origins. The sense of staggering is perfect here, suggesting both indecisiveness and motion backward and forward.

Yet, paradoxically, by glancing forward in time to his death, the speaker imagines returning to his first state. This suggestion of circularity is reinforced by the word *dust* (as in the biblical "dust to dust"):

And when this dust falls to the urn
In that state I came return.

The light that he would return to, the wholeness and completeness of that state, is there in the implied connection of tomb with womb. The headlong rush into time, helped on by the "black art" of sin, leads to the darkness of the grave. But by a wonderful kind of alchemy extremes meet. Darkness leads back to light, dust to new life, the urn to rebirth. The circle is complete:

the advance forward in time is also a "retreat" to the beginning. Eliot's phrase is pertinent here: "In my end is my beginning."

This turn, this "coincidence of contraries," to use the words of Nicolas of Cusa, gains even richer suggestions if we consider Vaughan's interest in alchemy (his brother Thomas was a Hermetic philosopher at Cambridge). Poems of the seventeenth century are rife with alchemical references that largely escape us today. In its higher form, alchemy, the search for the fabled philosopher's stone to transmute lead into gold, was a spiritual quest for wholeness. Though its material investigations led to modern chemistry, alchemy is perhaps best understood as a system of symbols of spiritual integration and transformation. Through its mysteries, qualities of mind, as well as things, might be transformed into their opposites—hence in "The Retreate" the transformation of darkness into the world of light, of dust into spirit. As in the Feyn diagram, the advance in time is the mirror image of the retreat. From the viewpoint of eternity, time may move in both directions at once, achieving balance and stasis. The couplet advances, but returns to end on the rhyme. In its end is its beginning.

The nostalgia for a childhood state of bliss, a condition of primordial harmony, suggests to the speaker the hope of final bliss after this life. The "bright shootes of everlastingnesse" felt by the child are hints akin to "sparks of fire out of the afflicted flint" experienced by the adult Vaughan. In each case, a thing is transformed into its opposite: mortal dress is invaded by bright shoots of everlastingness; cold flint becomes warm fire; time, as it advances, retreats to eternity.

What then, we may ask, is the value of life and time? Vaughan does not say, at least in this poem. In his much longer treatment of the subject, Wordsworth suggests that the value is the growth of the adult soul through the experience of separation and adversity:

The Clouds that gather round the setting sun
Do take a sober coloring from an eye
That hath kept watch o'er man's mortality;
Another race hath ben, and other palms are won.
Thanks to the human heart by which we live,
Thanks to its tenderness, its joys, and fears,
To me the meanest flower that blows can give
Thoughts that do often lie too deep for tears.

But for Vaughan in "The Retreate," the focus is that darkness, death, and time are finally transmuted into their contraries—light, life, and eternity.

One further consideration may assist in our response to Vaughan's poetry or Wordsworth's (or Traherne's or Blake's for that matter). In our empirical century it is difficult, except in physics, to question the process of time, to think of anything as not time-bound. Yet for Vaughan, as for Blake and Wordsworth after him, eternity was the natural magnet of the soul.

It may be, as many from the Orient have said, that we Westerners are bound up in the illusory web of appearances that the East calls *maya*. It is true we often seem too fascinated, or intimidated, by various reductionist systems of thought (most recently, perhaps, by forms of deconstruction) to feel comfortable asking the age-old questions concerning time and eternity. Yet the findings of subatomic physics in our century might well encourage us to do so, as matter itself appears increasingly to be simply one way of perceiving energy and to have no real substance in the usual sense of the word. Current models of matter are much closer to how we imagine energy, mind, or spirit to be than to the billiard-ball model of the atom that has dominated classical physics. Today when we hear a particle of matter defined as "the point of intersection of forces coterminous with the universe," or hear that String Theory posits six to eleven dimensions to explain the existence of a single atom, we realize that the old distinctions between mind and matter are much less clear.

In this developing climate of thought, it may be easier than before for us to entertain the vision of a Vaughan or a Wordsworth and to receive the intuitions they share from their recollections of childhood. According to at least one contemporary physicist, everything is conceivably composed of photons—in which case Vaughan's "world of light" may be the only world there is.

Author Biography

Robert Siegel is the author of seven books of poetry and fiction, including *The Beasts and the Elders, In a Pig's Eye,* and The *Whalesong* trilogy. His work has received awards from *Poetry* magazine, the Friends of Literature, the Ingram Foundation, and the National Endowment for the Arts as well as other sources. He has taught at Dartmouth and Princeton and at Goethe University in Frankfurt and is currently Professor of English at the University of Wisconsin-Milwaukee, where he has twice served as director of the graduate creative writing program.

In 1980, after my first book, *Turning*, was published, Clyde Kilby, a distinguished C. S. Lewis scholar and writing teacher, who had given me great encouragement with the work, suggested that I might want to get to know Madeleine L'Engle.

After all, we were both New Yorkers, he said.

I did not actually laugh, but I wanted to. The laughing would have been, first, because it was such a delightful suggestion, and, second, because it was (I felt sure) entirely out of the question. I had Madeleine L'Engle on a very high pedestal and there I thought she would remain.

Two (I suspect) providential events changed that. That same year, when I returned from New York City with my husband and family to my native New Orleans, I was signed up to do a press interview with Madeleine L'Engle. This very enlightening event took place over the long-distance wires, with L'Engle ensconced in her office at the Cathedral of St. John the Divine, and me leaning eagerly over the typewriter, discovering how easy she was to know, how quickly she moved from Lewis Carroll to the farthest reaches of the universe, how much I liked her ideas on writing (as well as the writing itself).

A few years later I met her in person at a meeting held high in the Colorado mountains, where a gathering of writers took place. It felt, to me, a bit like Mount Olympus, where the immortals might exchange ideas, sing songs, and enjoy one another's company.

Or, to use a southern expression of long standing, I thought I'd died and gone to heaven. Playing Ping-Pong in a three-way match with Luci Shaw and Madeleine L'Engle was an exquisite way to begin a professional friendship.

Meeting Madeleine L'Engle at that precise moment and

becoming one of a new circle of writers to which she extended friendship was encouraging. Her friendship and her example pointed my gaze to the beautiful, the sacred, the high adventure of creative life in the service of God.

As it turns out, Clyde Kilby was right.

Emilie Griffin

10
The Joyous Turn: Glimpsing Truth in Stories

Emilie Griffin

As a child, I loved stories. I did not know why I loved them, but I loved them. I wore out the librarian, Mrs. Wadsworth, at the Isidore Newman School, asking her to recommend another book like the one I had just read: one that would give me the same keen sense of knowing; the sudden pleasure of grasping the essence of things.

Books about dogs and horses were about the loss of home and the regaining of it; about devotion; about courage and heroism. Greek and Roman myths were about constancy, obedience, fidelity, courage. Orpheus was commanded not to look back as he led his beloved from the underworld; but he disobeyed and she vanished again into the land of the shades.

Most touching of all were the fairy tales. These, on a level I did not yet understand, were stories of hope and redemption.

In those days I did not take stories apart, trying to determine what made them work. Instead I let them wash over me, baptizing me in floods of understanding.

The best story by far took hold of me after high

school, when I received as a literary prize (for the best English essay) a copy of the King James Bible styled without chapter and verse numbers in order to be read as one might read any other book of stories: as literature. It was handsomely designed and beguiling in its preparation. Of course I had heard some Bible stories before. But now for the first time the stories (without chapter and verse citations to interrupt me) leapt off the page. Adam and Eve, Cain and Abel, Joseph and his brothers, Jacob and Leah and Rachel, David and Jonathan, Ruth and Naomi, Ruth and Boaz, all swept me away. The Bible was not, just at that moment, Holy Writ, to be revered and left on the shelf; but one mighty tale after another filled with hard-driving action, violence, romance, revealing all the errors of humanity: adulterous loves, insane dreams of conquest, sexual jealousy, murderous rages, anger, pride, lust, and all the rest. It was all about real life, a life that I had not yet experienced but meant to know more about one of these days.

I was also touched by stories of conversion: Abraham hearing and following God's call, Moses responding in spite of himself, Ruth promising to join Naomi's people. Such tales found answers in me, eager responses of Yes, I know, it has happened to me just that way.

I found out that Jesus was a fine storyteller and a better creative writing teacher than many. I learned that his stories spring from ordinary human experience. They touch our consciences. They keep us in suspense. Best of all, they connect us to the mysterious heart of God. What sort of Person, we want to know, would pay the same wages to the vineyard workers who came in late as to the ones who were there from the beginning of the day?

Now I know that when Jesus told stories, he was following the native theological tradition of his culture and society. Theology as we know it in the West—a brainy, intellectual affair—was simply unknown to the culture of Jesus. Theology was not merely embedded in story. Theology, for Hebrew/Judaic culture, was—and is—story. Narrative theology leads readily to narrative spirituality. The Gospel stories are not merely metaphors, but they disclose their metaphors in narrative style, one insight yielding to the next as the action unfolds. I do not mean to belittle the special gift that Jesus had; rather I want to emphasize how very Jewish of him it was to be such a fine storyteller.

For me, a certain kind of story has more than once led me into deeper wisdom. I mean the kind of story we sometimes call myth, and sometimes, fairy tale.

Once, while making a retreat in a converted Victorian mansion on a large country estate, I found myself remembering the story of Love and the Soul. In ancient Greek legend, the Soul, a lovely young woman, leaves her home (and her jealous older sisters) and goes to the palace of her unknown suitor. As she moves through the exquisite rooms, she hears beguiling music, finds appetizing foods and comfortable places of rest. At last her Lord, the Lord of Love, comes to her tenderly, but asks that she not inquire further about him or reveal his identity to anyone. In fact, he remains a mystery to her.

But the Soul, made curious by this request, lights a candle to watch him while he sleeps. Love, disappointed in her, rushes away. Many ancient folktales, from Western tradition and throughout the world, speak plainly to our human condition. They often tell us about our fearfulness and failure to trust. They remind us of a loving God who seeks our good, but also requires obedience: discipline.

Christian interpreters of fairy tales help us to tap into these deep sources of wisdom. David Steindl-Rast, a Benedictine monk, showed me how the fairy tale traces the path of holy obedience that the Christian is meant to follow. Whether it be Cinderella or Rapunzel or Snow

White, the fairy tale traces the path with a heart, the path of humility and trust . . . the path every believer is meant to pursue. Snow White shares our human condition. Three times she succumbs to temptation, submitting to the sinister and forbidden pleasures that fall into her path. She wears the colorful laces, and they choke her. In spite of all warnings against it, she uses the pretty comb. She eats the shining apple meant to destroy her. Each time she falls deeper into the sleep of death. Yet the tale of Snow White is all about resurrection. Love (the handsome prince) bends down and wakes her. The ending—the denouement—tells us that God's love is unconditional and will not be outwitted by death.

Comparing the story to St. Benedict's path of holy obedience, Steindl-Rast draws the parallel:

> "So let us then rise up at last," St. Benedict calls to his monks, "for Scripture is arousing us and saying it is high time for us to rise from sleep with eyes wide open to the light that makes us divine . . ." His words echo those of Ephesians (Eph 5:14): Awake, O sleeper, arise from the dead, and the Anointed One will shine on thee!
>
> When the monk comes against "impossible tasks," St. Benedict has one simple guideline: "out of love . . . in faith . . . let him obey." "Secure in hope" the monk journeys toward the goal. But this hope is truly open for surprise, not blocked by petty hopes. "For eye has not seen nor ear heard what God has prepared for those who love him."[1]

What awaits them is the unheard of, unseen lover, Love Himself.

A second Christian interpreter of fairy tale is Walter Wangerin, Jr., who speaks about the effects of his childhood encounter with Hans Christian Andersen.

Even so did Andersen's tales express what otherwise was mute in me. If I found my feelings in his stories, I was neither crazy nor alone. Someone shared my woe. Someone invited me to chuckle at it. Andersen gave me a frame for things intangible, bewildering, elemental, and urgent. Without apology he structured his world with things of spiritual value: the eternal consequences of actions good and evil, the judging and the benevolent presence of God, the effective reality of repentance, the marvelous power of divine forgiveness. These things surrounded me when I dwelt with him.[2]

Still another appreciation of fairy tale comes from one of its finest modern practitioners, J. R. R. Tolkien, philologist and author of the trilogy *The Lord of the Rings*. From him I learned that fairy stories are not for children but for adults.[3] And they exist to impart a great wisdom which comes from the deep wells of our experience.

Tolkien says that fairy tales are about the satisfaction of our greatest longings and desires. But even more important, he says, is the consolation of fairy tales. Fairy tales are about happy endings. That is precisely where fairy tales and Judeo-Christian stories intersect. The story of Moses is a story of consolation and renewal. The story of Daniel is a story of rescue. The story of Jesus bears within it the greatest possible happy ending: our own salvation and our ultimate arrival on the blessed shores.

> The consolation of fairy stories . . . the joy of the happy ending . . . is a sudden and miraculous grace: never to be counted on to recur. It does not deny the existence . . . of sorrow and failure . . . the possibility of these is necessary to the joy of deliverance; it denies . . . universal final defeat and in so far is *evangelium* . . . giving a fleeting glimpse of Joy, Joy beyond the walls of the world, poignant as grief.[4]

Tolkien goes further. Having traced the nature of fairy story, he makes the direct comparison to the Christian story and drives the point home: this story has entered and transformed our world. The birth of Christ, the incarnation and redemption, the resurrection . . . this is *the joyous turn,* the story that begins and ends in joy. Tolkien says, "The Christian joy, the *Gloria,* is of the same kind: but it is preeminently high and joyous. Because this story is supreme: and it is true."

We treasure the happy endings, especially when they convince us. For we know that (on this side of the boundary, at least) happy endings are not guaranteed. For love to be precious, it must be precarious. The best stories are about risk and danger. They entertain the possibility of loss and failure. They acquaint us with grief. Stories that are rigged to turn out favorably are lifeless, unsatisfying. With the loss of persuasion comes a loss of interest. We tire, we riffle the pages, we close the book and let it fall.

I chose my vocation as writer before I had clearly chosen the Christian path, although indeed, as I now see, I was on the path before I knew where it was leading. I wanted to write because of the way stories had affected me. At first, the particular form of storytelling that attracted me was drama. At the performance of plays in darkened theaters I had felt again that breakthrough moment remembered from childhood, when reality pours through suddenly, provoking us to tears or laughter—because of heightened perception, an awakening.

Something else I learned about narrative in the theater: how the audience acts in the unfolding of the story. It could be argued, no doubt it has been argued, that the audience is as much a character in the story as the characters on stage. The audience identifies with some person on stage and takes his or her part against adversaries, murmuring with anticipation and fear when some fall or misfortune is about to happen.

As I sat in the theater, watching a Broadway performance of Samuel Beckett's nihilistic play, *Waiting for Go-
dot,* I was startled by my own sense of the truth of God
working through the play and through the performers.
Bert Lahr, playing a tramp, came downstage and held
the audience spellbound as he ate a carrot, then sprayed
a fine rain of carrot fragments through the air. His su-
perb clowning, the compassion and charm of his acting,
bore witness to a divine spark in him and in the play.
Like a child at a puppet show who wants to alert the
chicken to the presence of Reynard the Fox, I wanted
to call out to those characters who could not find God,
"God is right there on stage with you, if only you knew!"

Madeleine L'Engle records a similar experience having
to do with one of Eugene Ionesco's plays, *The Chairs,*
in which an elderly couple living on a small island spend
the time span of the play waiting for a man who will
come to bring them a message about the meaning of
life:

> As I remember the play (which I saw a good many
> years ago) the old man and woman keep shifting
> chairs about, while the sharks swim outside. At the
> very end of the play a man comes on stage, dressed
> in top hat and tails, and unrolls a script on which is
> written the meaning of life, and he mumbles:
> Anhhh . . . unhhh . . . aunh . . .

L'Engle is outraged. She refuses to accept the play-
wright's apparently nihilistic conclusion (though she
does allow him an alternative interpretation, that Ionesco may be saying it is pride for any human being to
presume to give others the key to life's meaning). But
at the same time she acknowledges the art of the absurd:

> The art of the absurd can, indeed, be revelatory, as
> in Ionesco's *Rhinoceros,* which is an icon, an affirma-

tion of the value of being fully human, and so an affirmation of incarnation. But sometimes it can lead into madness.[5]

Can it be (as L'Engle suggests, and I also felt to be so) that God is acting through the conscience of his people who as audience may judge the truth or untruth of what happens in the play? Actors know well the power of the audience. They sense the difference between rehearsal and performance. They wait, apprehensively but eagerly, for an audience to bring the play alive, judging yet encouraging, with laughter, applause, boos, and hisses, even the sudden draw of breath that signals alarm at what is about to happen. And God is telling his story through the audience as well, when the moral concerns of the audience bring truth to light. They know the nature of humanity. They know that marital inconstancy will have its consequences, that murder will out.

Does God speak through writers who are not professed believers? It has been my experience that God speaks in most unexpected ways. In my early days as a seeker of faith I learned, much to my amazement, how God can speak through apparently secular stories to call us deeper into faith.

In his imaginative novel *Was,* Geoff Ryman reveals to us both the depth of our longing for heaven and the revelatory power of story. Ryman does not celebrate belief. He proclaims no evangelium. Yet his faithfulness to his own vision results in a provocative interweaving of four distinct but related stories and locales: the intersections of the lives of Judy Garland, Frank Baum (author of the *Wonderful Wizard of Oz*), the mystical Dorothy Gale of his story, the historical Dorothy Gael from whose unhappiness the tale is fashioned, and a man named Jonathan who is dying of AIDS. The landscapes are the stuff of folklore: Los Angeles, California, and Manhattan, Kansas. Ryman persuades me again of what I already know: all country is heart country.

Ryman's long-suffering hero, Jonathan, is thirty-eight and knows he will not live to see the year 2000. To me, as a believer, his emptiness, as with many of the book's characters, seems like a failure to know that he is deeply loved by God. This is the hollowness of the book. Its chilling ironies are jokes against God. Aunty Em's religious zeal is a mockery; Uncle Henry's sexual history is heartbreak; across the American landscape there is no sign of Glinda the Good Witch of the North. These are T. S. Eliot's hollow men and women, their heads and bodies stuffed with straw. The Kansas wind whistles through them.

Yet with Ryman's hammer strokes of fantasy profound meanings are driven through. A dying Jonathan looks for heaven not only in Kansas but on the fields adjacent to Dorothy's farm. And in what can only be called a mystical transformation, he vanishes from sight. Bill, who has accompanied the dying man into the fields and wants to understand his disappearance, is driven back into miracle:

> He saw rainbows, a corridor of them all along the valley, parallel to the hills, lined up over the straight, flat Kansas road. On his right he saw the sun, and all the sky there had flared orange. This is the rainbow, he thought, for that is what it looks like when you stand in a rainbow. For someone else.
>
> "Oh, Jesus," he murmured, in astonishment, in wonder. He started to pray and found he didn't have to. Kansas prayed for him. . . .
>
> After a lifetime of prayer, Bill Davison had finally had a vision. Of God?[26]

It is an almost unrecognizable Christian vision (unrecognizable to those of us who happily sing our way through "Jesus loves me, this I know"), but Jesus Christ is present here nonetheless, appearing even to the tortured Dorothy as the Child the wise men followed, now crucified by human distortions. In this twisted fairy tale (really four tales in one, constructed as ingeniously as three-dimensional chess) we may look hard and in vain for Tolkien's joyous turn. God is present, even so.

Where there is truth, where there are stories, God is there. Over the whole storytelling enterprise God arches with covenantal power and bends down to us with tenderness. We seek this God by hearing stories, reading them, researching them, telling them. As Jonathan, who has traveled to Manhattan, Kansas, to research the real Dorothy Gael, says in his letter of farewell, "All this search for history was a search for home."[7]

Now I am convinced that the presence of God may be discerned in the most unlikely narratives. What is needed for this Godspying, however, is a special kind of grace, a bounty God gives us not because we deserve or have earned it, but merely because we desire it. God is the master storyteller. In stories God shows himself to us in godly places as well as in the rubble of ungodly ones.

Author Biography

Emilie Griffin has written six books on spiritual life, including *Turning* (about conversion), *Clinging* (about prayer), *Chasing the Kingdom: A Parable of Faith*, *The Reflective Executive* (about spirituality in business life), *Homeward Voyage: Reflections on Life-Changes*, and the very recent *Wilderness Time: The Experience of Retreat*.

A professional writer, editor, and marketing consultant, Emilie has won fifty awards for creativity. She has worked extensively as a retreat and workshop leader with Christians of all denominations and is a member of the board of RENO-VARE, an infra-church movement committed to Christian renewal.

Emilie and her husband, William Griffin, were founding members of the Chrysostom Society, a Christian writers group formed in the1980s. They are also members of the Catholic Commission on Intellectual and Cultural Affairs. They live in New Orleans and are the parents of three grown children.

When my book *Presenting Madeleine L'Engle* was published in 1992 (Twayne/Macmillan), I was introduced to the kinds of attacks that Madeleine has suffered for years, including some rather similar to the surreal scenario that leads off my essay. I rarely recognized the Madeleine described in these attacks. The person these Christians were attacking was not the person I had met or the author of the books I had written about. These critics rarely understood the ways that fiction conveys meaning, and they held, I believe, a rather narrow view of what Christian fiction should look like. So my intention here is to nibble away at the subject, to talk a bit about Madeleine's fiction in an extended conversation about the nature of fiction that embodies Christian faith.

Donald R. Hettinga

11
A Great Cloud of Witnesses

Donald R. Hettinga

It probably would not surprise anyone if I were to begin by saying that through my reading of Madeleine L'Engle's fiction I have found myself in unusual worlds. It is a commonplace of fantasy fiction that readers depart this world for the pleasures and problems of other realms. But what has surprised me is that these trips are not to realms of L'Engle's creation. What happens is this: I feel myself transported through time and place—not to Uriel where in *A Wrinkle in Time* glorious creatures sing continuous praise to God their maker, nor to the orb in *A Swiftly Tilting Planet* where time-traveling unicorns are hatched to drink and serve the wind. The place I arrive has more of the feel of that seventeenth-century village where a Pastor Mortmain stirred a cauldron of hate and suspicion. Yet while the emotional atmosphere matches L'Engle's account of that witch-hunt, the setting I find myself in is much more modern.

The walls are heavily paneled in dark walnut. I sit in a leather chair behind a long oak table and face my interrogators on the panel of the House Committee on Un-American Activities. To the side is a gallery of photographers, with flashbulbs poised to capture my response to the question that echoes from Senator McCarthy: "Are you now or have you ever been an advocate of Madeleine L'Engle's fiction?"

Before I can answer, the walls morph back from walnut to the pastel concrete of more familiar environs, a college classroom or a church multi-purpose room, and I find myself in what is too often a reality—a room full of Christian readers who believe or have been told to believe that one of our most significant contemporary writers—a writer who professes to that same faith they profess—is a dangerous heretic.

Should we be cross with people for taking her books so seriously? I do not think so. We might be cross with their bad readings of her books and cross with their less than charitable discourse about her books and her person but not with the fact that they are taking them seriously. It is ludicrous for defenders of literature to say, as they sometimes do in the midst of a controversy, "Oh, it's just a book. It's only a story. It's not going to hurt anyone." Books *do* change people's lives. Stories *do* matter. And so we ought to care about the legacy of any books, any stories. We ought to think carefully about the worlds we enter, the characters and values we entertain there and that entertain us.

My students these days would be very quick to point out that whether or not the child cares about the source of the magic in a book, we (we who write, guide, teach, evaluate, etc.) ought to. And they would be right, of course, particularly in speaking about those of us who participate in Christian communities and particularly when we are talking about a writer like L'Engle who gives us books that show us something about the nature of the universe as well as something about the nature of God in relation to that universe. She has said repeatedly what she said early on in *A Circle of Quiet*, that "one cannot discuss structure in writing without discussing structure in all life; it is impossible to talk about why anybody writes a book or paints a picture or composes a symphony without talking about the nature of the universe."[1] And her critics on the evangelical right are quick to remind their audiences that L'Engle's fantasy fiction is susceptible to theological inquisition because she herself writes that her fantasy is her theology.

That being the case, should not we Christians garland ourselves with garlic (or at least put on the spectacles of scripture) before picking up these books bearing the images of demonic heads and astral spirit guides, not to mention New Age symbols like rainbows and unicorns? And when we hear from others or when we come upon a page in *A Wrinkle in Time* that mentions Jesus as well as Einstein, Buddha, Schweitzer, Curie, and others as fighters on the same team against evil, should not we cry for censorship or simply—as an elementary teacher in my city did—stop reading the book, telling ourselves or our audience (a fourth-grade class in this example) that this book is a bad book because it misrepresents God. After all, not only does Jesus himself suggest that it would be better for any of us to take a dip with a millstone than to mislead a young person about God; even the patriarch of Western democracy— Plato—suggests that books that might mislead young people about the nature of the gods should be censored in his ideal republic.

Yet, I would assert that when we think carefully about the worlds that L'Engle has given us, we see an array of worlds—fantastic or otherwise—that mirror the problems and possibilities of our own. And if we reflect on those worlds we can see, I believe, a lengthy queue of characters who embody Christian values. Antagonistic readers have made much of L'Engle's comment that her fantasies are her theology, coming to her fiction then with the expectation that the novels can be read like volumes of systematic theology, and, of course, such readers are then perplexed or put off by the characters and events of the fiction that live and breathe, succeed and fail, dream and despair according to the fictional realities of the works of art in which they appear. Yet if we look at the examples of the characters in that queue we can see evidence of a theology that centers on a triune, sovereign but loving God, who calls believers to an active role in a cosmic battle against evil, but who forgives them when they fail and atones for their failure with the substitutionary sacrifice of the eternal Christ. In short, if we read the novels as novels, and not as theological discourse, and if we approach them with openness instead of with the mindset of prosecuting attorneys, we can see a fairly orthodox, evangelical Christian worldview; we can see, I think, what L'Engle in *Walking on Water* said that we ought to be able to see in the corpus of a writer who is a Christian—not a certifiable number of references to Jesus, not characters that live exemplary Christian lives, but a clear vision of what that writer believes about God and the nature of the universe.

Think about the worlds that we enter in the time trilogy. Fantasy, L'Engle has said, gives her the opportunity to talk about the way the world ought to be as well as the way that it is, and so she can show us the creation both before the fall and after. Why, in *A Wrinkle in Time*, do the questors need to stop on the planet Uriel before encountering the evil that has imprisoned Mr. Murry on the planet Camazotz? Quite simply, the protagonists and the readers need to see the nature of good in order to fully comprehend the magnitude of evil. But it is the nature of this Edenic planet that speaks much about L'Engle's view of creation. Here the created beings and, indeed, the very planet itself sing continuous praise and thanksgiving to their creator. The closest translation for humans, readers learn, is a triumphant psalm from Isaiah 42.

But that music and dance do not just appear in this

one novel. Whenever L'Engle wants readers to see the world the way it ought to be, she uses this music that is akin to the medieval concept of the music of the spheres—a music and dance that embodies both the harmonies and goodness of creation and simultaneously glorifies the Creator. It is the sound of the obedient Sporos within the mitochondrion in *A Wind in the Door;* it is the healing dance of the dolphins in *A Ring of Endless Light;* it is the sound of the stars in *Many Waters* and the sound of the wind in *A Swiftly Tilting Planet.* These fictional worlds suggest an author who believes that a good God created a world that was good.

But if in the theology of L'Engle's fiction the world originally was created good, it has also clearly fallen and is under attack by forces of evil, which, though they do not conform to the pop-medieval stereotypes of Frank Peretti's fiction, do embody real spiritual forces. The Murrays, the O'Keefes, the Austins, the Reniers—and even Camilla Dickinson and Katherine Vigneras—do not in their various plots and adventures battle simply against flesh and blood, or even against phobias, repressions, and insecurities, but against powers and principalities that are actively involved in the business of the physical realm.

These powers work to negate God's work. If God's work is creation and affirmation—he makes *and names* his creatures—then the work of his antithesis is negation, getting created beings to deny their identity as creatures of God. After all, the word *diabolical* means "to tear apart." Such is the work of the black thing in *A Wrinkle in Time* that transforms creatures from individuals with unique gifts and peculiarities, individuals motivated by love and thanksgiving, to robotic automatons who lack consciousness, passion, and emotion. Such is the work of the Echthroi—the fallen angels—in *A Wind in the Door* and in *A Swiftly Tilting Planet* that offer false visions of reality to pull victims into a nothingness.

Such is the work of the nephilim in *Many Waters*. Such is the work of the spirits of hurt and bitterness that harden Polly O'Keefe's heart in *A House Like a Lotus*. Such is the work of the spirits of hate and despair that attack Vicky Austin in *The Moon by Night* and in *A Ring of Endless Light*, and Stella Renier in *The Other Side of the Sun*. If, as so many L'Engle characters discover, God has numbered all his creation, the forces of evil like nothing better than to play math games with what he has numbered, math games that use zero as a multiplier, math games that leave their victims wondering what Vicky Austin is wondering in this passage from *A Ring of Endless Light:* "What for? Why be conscious in a world like this? Why bother/it doesn't matter/because nothing matters."[2]

A part of the power of L'Engle's portrayal of this cosmic battle is her refusal to let battle be simply cosmic or merely spiritual. Instead, the spiritual attacks come in very real circumstances, in situations that mirror the complexity of human experience and the ambivalent impulses of an individual psyche. Meg Murry is tempted with what she always wanted—to simply fit in, to have a world where everything is normal. Charles Wallace Murry is tempted to hubris because of his native gifts of extraordinary intelligence and extra-sensory perception. The Echthroi and the nephilim tempt their victims with the pleasurable swirl of hedonism, a temptation that L'Engle's fiction suggests (in metaphorical terms that any evangelical Christian would recognize) is a natural developmental stage: "The temptation for farandola or for man or for star is to stay an immature pleasure seeker," declares the cherubim Proginoskes in *A Wind in the Door*. "When we seek our own pleasure as the ultimate good we place ourselves as the center of the universe. A fara or a man or a star has his place in the universe, but nothing created us the center."[3]

One danger faced by any author portraying such cosmic conflicts is that the conventions of the genre coupled with the belief in a moral dichotomy tempt the author into creating characters that are flat, into drafting plots that are predictable, plots that, as reviewer George Woods complains about other fantasy writers, try too hard to pass along a moral message: "When you start reading the books, you find one damn quest after another. It's always the battle between good and evil, between the forces of light and dark—forever. As soon as the hero finishes one quest, he's given another one."[4] While the quests in L'Engle's novels are many, L'Engle avoids the repetitiousness of which Wood complains in part by creating characters that are troubled by pain or have doubts that compete with their faith. When Polly O'Keefe is challenged about her beliefs in *An Acceptable Time*, she realizes that she has no well-packaged answers for her questioner; "I don't know, either," she acknowledges, "about the Creator I believe made everything."[5] But it is exactly this dimension of doubt in a character, this kind of questioning, that allows L'Engle's fiction to move beyond fantasy formulas. Polly's admission that she "felt nothing but rebellion" in her own heart and her honest questioning of Christ's presence in the midst of her own difficulties make her character credible to contemporary readers in a way that a more self-assured expression of faith might not. Her complex feelings here make her subsequent acceptance of Christ's sacrifice all the more powerful: "A thousand years away, that blood had been freely given. That was enough. She did not have to understand."[6] By creating a Polly who believes but cannot quite understand her beliefs, or a Stella Renier who is an atheist forced to acknowledge the reality of powers and principalities beyond the empirical world, or a Camilla Dickinson who is called upon to exercise love in the face of overwhelming evil and brokenness, L'Engle takes readers beyond the banalities of the formulaic fiction that too many writers, Christian or otherwise, succumb to.

But in crafting such characters is L'Engle simply showing, as some fundamentalist Christian readers might say, her true colors? Is not this what we might expect from someone who has an office in the Cathedral of St. John the Divine? And in praising such portrayals of ambivalent faith are we falling prey to a modernist aesthetic that privileges doubt over certainty? I think not. It seems to me, rather, that the governing aesthetic principle behind both the creation of the characters and an appreciation of the stories of such characters is honesty.

If we believe that one obligation of the writer who is also a Christian is to tell the truth, then the truth has to include Christians who, like Polly, find themselves sometimes overwhelmed in the midst of crisis and somehow unable to articulate what they believe. And if we believe in this responsibility to tell the truth, we must recognize that the truth includes Christians like Pastor Mortmain in *A Swiftly Tilting Planet* who exercise all sorts of evil under the banner of Christ, and that it includes nonbelievers like Joshua in *The Arm of the Starfish* who do the work of Christ even when they find it impossible to profess the tenets of an organized religion.

Moreover, if we hope that one result of fiction written by writers who are Christians is that readers of all ilks might see the truth, the power, and the possibilities of God's kingdom, then we need to seriously consider how this kind of truth-telling about characters might serve that purpose. L'Engle's *The Other Side of the Sun* presents an excellent opportunity to see how an honest portrayal of characters in all of their various stages of faith or doubt and confusion of faith can present a powerfully Christian view of the world and of the nature of good and evil even though the protagonist professes to be an atheist and even though she never prays "the sinner's prayer."

The world that Stella Renier, the daughter of an Oxford philosopher, enters when she joins her new husband's family in an isolated coastal community in the southern United States is as alien to most contemporary readers as it was to her. It is alien in part because of the social setting, a time and place in which the wounds of the Civil War were still festering, a world in which African-American vigilante riders coursed the night in unhappy mimicry of white-hooded Ku Klux Klan riders. But more significantly, it is alien because of the spiritual landscape of the southern United States, a landscape in which voodoo haunts the swamps that surround the Christian community, a landscape in which a parasol-bearing Anglican white woman will drive her buggy into the scrub to consult a black fortune-teller she considers less than human, a landscape in which a Bible-believing black woman, brought to America by a white slaver, can hold on to the promises of the Scripture but can still feel the pull of the tarot cards and the African magic from her past. For a Christian writer not named O'Connor to place an empirically educated character in such a setting in a novel published by a secular publishing house a handful of years after a national magazine told popular culture that God was dead takes a bit of chutzpa.

Is this what L'Engle meant in *Walking on Water* when she said that she wanted to create for her readers art that "shows a light so Lovely that they want with all their hearts to know the source of it"?[7] This is a novel in which one group of nominal Christians plans a mass kidnapping to ship black citizens to Africa on a flotilla of white-owned pleasure craft, and this is a novel that chronicles the failure of a more sincerely crafted Christian community designed to redress the evils of slavery. This is a novel in which the heroine apparently saves her unborn baby only by flinging a voodoo doll into a fire. This is a novel in which one of the figures of virtue, an elderly aunt of Stella's, shoots, at a climactic moment, a young black man that she loves as a son in order to prevent his lynching by Klansmen. This is a novel that shows virtuous action rewarded with death, that presents the family as a repository of silliness, a nest of bickering best avoided by the sensible, heroic characters.

Would it not have been a better witness to the faith if L'Engle had focused on the kind of family that prayed together as it faced difficulties, a family firmly grounded in Scripture? Why show Nyssa, a failed Christian community, instead of a successful mission? Would it not have been better if Stella could have quoted the words of Christ to save her from the voodoo, if she could have exercised spiritual authority over the demons attacking her and bound them in the name of Jesus? Would it not have been a clearer testimony if Honoria, the ex-wife of the slaver, had burned her tarot cards and had nothing to do with things of darkness? Why show Clive, Honoria's current husband, always standing with his Bible, yet impotent to protect anyone? And why have Aunt Olivia kill Ron? Why have a character break one of the Lord's commandments and try to twist it into heroism, into an act of love? How does that show that "we can do all things through Christ who strengthens us"?

The answer to this latter question and to most of the others is that these events show exactly how we can do all things through Christ, with an emphasis on the plural personal pronoun *we*. The novel suggests that it is not simply one person who can do all things in the power of Christ—that would imply a kind of perfection that is not feasible. The "witness" of such a fiction would be, I think, a rather destructive one. Christian readers would see how far they fall short of such perfection and would feel condemned by the ideal held out by the novel. Non-Christian readers would observe the disjunction between reality and the world of the novel and be quick to remark on what to them would appear as yet another instance of Christian hypocrisy. What we see instead are individuals who might fail as they try to act upon their faith but individuals who act, nonetheless, and whose collective actions reveal something of how individual gifts and actions complement each other within the body of Christ.

The witness of such a fiction is honest and, hence, more powerful. Christian readers can see the results of passivity and the dangers of fear. They can see how Olivia's lack of action early on may have contributed to the horrific scene in which she kills Ron. They can see how Stella's fear of commitment brings great danger to the community and to her unborn child. They can see, in short, that each individual must choose between action on behalf of what is good and action on behalf of what is evil. Not to choose *is* to choose for evil or, at least, to open the door to evil. The theme is a consistent one in L'Engle's work. Stella Renier cannot pretend that the voodoo and the racist riders do not exist any more than Polly O'Keefe can ignore the human sacrifice in *An Acceptable Time* or Adam Eddington the evil conspiracy in *The Arm of the Starfish*. Non-Christian readers can see the power of faith as James, Honoria, Clive, Ron, and Stella strive against the manifestations of evil. The plausibility of their personal struggles makes their ultimate victory more convincing.

Fiction must tell the truth. Fiction written by Christians ought to tell the truth about the brokenness in the world, *and* it ought to give us a glimpse of what it will mean for the lion to lie down with the lamb. Yet it ought to, as Katherine Paterson has said, show us that "hope is more than happiness"; it ought to, as this novel suggests (as, really, all of L'Engle's fiction suggests), show us that "only on love's terrible other side is found the place where lion and lamb abide." Christian fiction can display the glory of God's creation, the treasure of God's grace, but it can only honestly do so in earthen vessels. We can see the cracks in the facades of these characters, but we can also see the glory of God's light shining through them. That is what L'Engle gives us in Stella and Meg, in Felix and Frank, in Canon Tallis and Bishop Colubra. And that is L'Engle's gift.

The gift that L'Engle gives us in these earthen vessels, the gift that she presents to us through this "great cloud of witnesses," is that of St. Paul's assurance that although we who are sons and daughters of God may be "hard pressed on every side," we will not be "crushed." The gift is that of Lancelot Andrews's assertion in L'Engle's recent novel that "all the wickedness in the world which man may do or think is no more to the mercy of God than a live coal dropped in the sea." The gift is L'Engle's reminder that we, like Vicky Austin, are caught and held within a ring of endless light.

Author Biography

Donald R. Hettinga lives in western Michigan, where he teaches children's literature and writing at Calvin College. He is the author of several books including *Presenting Madeleine L'Engle, Sitting at the Feet of the Past: Retelling the North American Folktale for Children, In the World: Reading and Writing as a Christian* and has edited a volume on British children's literature in the *Dictionary of Literary Biography*. He is currently working on a biography of Jacob and Wilhelm Grimm for which he received the 1998 Ezra Jack Keats DeGrummond Fellowship.

I first heard Madeleine speak in chapel at Wheaton College while I was researching my Chesterton biography at the college's Wade Center (which houses the papers of Chesterton, Lewis, Sayers, and others). We met again at the Illinois Wesleyan University Writers' Conference in 1982 when I interviewed Madeleine for *The Episcopalian* and was thrilled to hear that she had read my Chesterton book in page proofs and liked it even better than my Sayers biography. We discovered a mutual affection for the works of L. M. Montgomery: *Anne of Green Gables* and *Emily of New Moon,* and as dog lovers, shared our disapproval of C. S. Lewis's idea that our four-footed friends live on only in our memories. Since then we have met at Mundelein College for picnic lunches or at De Koven on retreat, while maintaining our friendship by letter, an appropriate way for Sayers's admirers to interact.

Alzina Stone Dale

12
The Lives of the Saints: Twentieth-Century Style

Alzina Stone Dale

As a biographer who believes that the lives and works of artists are inextricably intertwined, I have found it fascinating to compare the lives of two well-known twentieth-century writers, Madeleine L'Engle and Dorothy L. Sayers. They have both been role models for me, and I believe they will also make valuable mentors for women in the next millennium.

Their lives stretch from the end of the nineteenth century to the beginnings of the twenty-first. Dorothy L. Sayers was born in 1893, became a published author in the 1920s, and died in 1957 about the century's midpoint. Her life overlapped by about a dozen years the time when L'Engle had graduated from college and published her first novel, *The Small Rain*, and as the century closes, L'Engle is still very much with us.

Neither woman has consciously patterned herself on the other, but their lives are based not only on similar ambitions but on similar beliefs, making them surprisingly alike. When I first suggested this to L'Engle fifteen years ago, she modestly demurred, but I believe it is no coincidence that since that time, she has not only continued to publish religious essays and autobiographical pieces that relate art to the Christian life, but also was asked to write introductions to Dorothy L. Sayers's *The Mind of the Maker* and C. S. Lewis's *A Grief Observed.*

I do not mean that the lives of these two creative, amusing, and outspoken women are identical. At mid-century it became Sayers's job to proclaim the Good News in modern language to those of us who scarcely knew it. A generation later, however, L'Engle's task was to restore to believers the right to doubt and argue, quoting, as I heard her do, from T. S. Eliot's J. Alfred Prufrock's "Do I dare / Disturb the universe?" Their differing approaches demonstrate what Sayers called the "dialectic in Christian art which impels it to stress . . . now the eternal . . . now the temporal elements in the Divine drama."

Both women have been accused of "modernity," the kind of accusation history usually reverses without the individual's changing at all. But both were ahead of the time in trying to make the story/drama accessible. L'Engle's use of a genderless *el* as a name for God predates the current rage for inclusiveness, just as Sayers's translation of the Gospels in *The Man Born to Be King* preceded the multitude of contemporary translations.

Once groups like the Protestant Truth Society publicly accused Sayers of profaning the very name of God in her radio plays. Now Sayers is criticized by feminist Ann Loades for showing no interest in gender-inclusive language and for being a markedly conservative theologian! In L'Engle's case her accusers have called her a "New Age" priestess who questions "eternal verities" because, as her publisher Stephen Board wrote, "her writings venture into theology and the Bible in exploratory and unconventional ways . . . [although] in beliefs she stands within the broad tradition of . . . creeds and doctrine. . . ."

The only biography of L'Engle, Carole F. Chase's

Madeleine L'Engle, Suncatcher, called L'Engle a mystic. Chase assumed a timelessness, not growth, in L'Engle's career and emphasized themes rather than her evolving life and work. Chase did not refer to the role L'Engle played within the Episcopal Church during a tumultuous period, not by joining the radicals nor by choosing the priesthood, but by doing things long considered "men's work," such as preaching and leading retreats. L'Engle chose a middle ground: standing firm for her beliefs but not interrupting her vocation as a writer to hop on a bus to protest something. As a result, like Sayers, L'Engle has continued to have a wide readership of admirers, many women, for whom she is still a notable model for a woman's right to choose her own vocation.

Most important of all, L'Engle, like Sayers, does not consider herself a theologian. Both are—and always have been—writers. L'Engle insists that she is an artist for whom Story is paramount. If you substitute the term *Drama* for *Story,* you have the same affirmation from Sayers, who ended her career translating Dante because she so admired his storytelling and wanted to share it with her world. For them, story/drama is the basis for the faith itself, for as Sayers wrote in *The Man Born to Be King,* the Christian story is "a true story, the turning-point of history, the only thing that has really happened."

But both "makers and craftsmen" become very angry when their work is said to "do good" because, as Sayers commented, "it is dangerous for anybody—even the Church—to urge artists to produce works of art for the . . . purpose of doing good to people . . . this pseudo-art does not really communicate power to us; it exerts power over us . . . the only Christian work is good work well done." L'Engle wrote that "when the artist is truly the servant of the work, the work is better than the artist . . . to paint a picture or write a story is an incarnational activity."[1]

As an adult, Sayers refused to work at church fetes, but she put a lot of time and effort into being a church warden, an uncommon role for women in the 1950s. L'Engle had run a church choir and had put on pageants and plays before she took on the equally unusual role of leading retreats and beginning to preach. Living as we do in a period when society urges women to be "as good as a man," proving it by breaking the glass ceiling or competing in armed combat, Sayers's comment, with which L'Engle would agree, is fitting for us to consider: ". . . a woman is just as much an ordinary human being as a man with the same individual preferences . . . and what is repugnant to every human being is to be reckoned always as a member of a class and not as an individual person." Instead of reconstituting society to worship the Earth Mother, whose gospel demands that women run the universe, Sayers's words point to the conclusion that what contemporary women need is mentors who have lived with grace as individuals.

How did L'Engle and Sayers come to be such? The basic clue lies in the parallels in their lives. Both were cradle Christians, whose Anglican nurture included the golden gift of two great classics of the English language: the King James Bible and the Book of Common Prayer. This upbringing fostered their strong sense of continuity with the past. I once heard L'Engle tell a large audience of writers and teachers that by abandoning the King James Bible, we were taking away our children's birthright: their *mother* tongue.

Indeed, in her introduction to Sayers's *The Mind of the Maker,* L'Engle wisely commented that despite Sayers's initial disclaimers, she did not believe that her book could have been written by one who was not a totally committed Christian. This insight of L'Engle's applies to her own work as well. Neither wanted the label *"Christian* writer" any more than the label *"woman* writer," but their writing does reflect their deeply held beliefs.

Their best-known work—Sayers's detective stories and L'Engle's children's books—are widely read by nonbelievers, carrying the Christian message to churched and unchurched alike.

In spite of today's superior attitude, which assumes that mothers of a previous generation were barefoot in the kitchen, both these writers regarded their mothers as vital to their self-esteem and their careers, and were grateful that their mothers determined that they use their remarkable talents. Both were only children, too, which meant that their parents' attention was focused upon them, but also that they were thrown upon their own imaginations for friendship and entertainment, fostering their early development as writers.

Both were bookworms in families of readers. Sayers, however, adored *The Three Musketeers*, which led to the creation of Lord Peter Wimsey. L'Engle's great love was *Emily of New Moon* by the author of *Anne of Green Gables*, in which the heroine was an introspective, journal-keeping would-be writer. School was no problem academically for either, and both had university educations at a time when that opportunity was not automatically given to girls. Both wrote and published work at an early age. Although she had written stories and plays, Sayers's first published work was poetry, which was also to be her last love, while L'Engle has been a lifelong poet. Gawky in adolescence, both achieved a degree of inner confidence, but neither affected the romantic image of the self-centered "portrait of the artist as a young man," because it was neither practical nor suited to their belief that the artist is the servant of the work.

Both, too, were letter writers and journal keepers. Writing letters was Dorothy L. Sayers's favorite occupation, by which she kept in touch and shared her life and work with her family and friends. L'Engle's journals originally were a private expression of ideas, emotions, and events, but now serve as the grist for letters to friends as well as sources for future writing and lecturing.

Both adored the theater from an early age and liked to act as well as write for the stage. As an adult, Sayers found in the theater the kind of community and sense of common purpose a church of her time ought to have had, but seldom did. For L'Engle, having been an actress, writing and producing plays of her own, as well as having a professional actor for a husband, the world of the theater has long been an integral part of her creative life.

Although busy professionals, both had personal responsibility for their parents, husbands, and children, together with a multitude of other obligations such as writers' organizations throughout their lives. They recognized that these relationships were a part of life and in their fiction and essays discussed them as real-life issues. Working at home as they both did for years, the two also managed to keep the inevitable distractions under control, in return for space (and time) to work, but it would be hard to describe either of them as "coddled" in that respect.

On the other hand, many writers have been comforted in their own struggles to combine public and private lives by L'Engle's description of her own in *A Circle of Quiet* and *The Summer of the Great Grandmother.* Sayers had plenty of troubles in her life, too, but her humorous buoyancy kept her afloat, as shown in a 1939 letter to Muriel Byrne called "A Day in the Life of an Inoffensive Citizen." In it Sayers detailed a day spent trying to hire a housemaid, dictate letters to her secretary, find a carpenter, answer the door, take tea with her husband, all the while brooding over writing a piece to be a "Christmas message to the nation."

Unlike L'Engle's writings where families abound, there are not many children in Sayers's works. But in her play

Love All, the heroine Janet Reed insisted that for a child it was better to have a mother who was doing what she did best (writing plays) than an unhappy housewife, just as time spent coddling a male writer was not as fulfilling as being one herself.

In L'Engle's *A Wrinkle In Time,* the wife and mother is the working partner of the husband and father, but like so many L'Engle mothers, she is also the chief cook and bottlewasher. (By World War II housemaids were not just rare; they were extinct, and families like mine with a professor mother learned a lot of household skills.) But as an adult, I have found it helpful to recall L'Engle saying that it would keep our feet on the ground to come home from a book signing to have our children ask, "What's for supper?"

How to combine parenting and profession is a major challenge for the twenty-first century, when "having it all" leaves many women ragged and resentful. Both Sayers and L'Engle suggest "community" as a solution—not quite the Hillary Clinton "village," but work done within a committed group like the theater or a religious order. Both have written descriptions of such a group, like the order run by L'Engle's intriguing Mother Superior Catherine of Sienna in *The Severed Wasp.* She was creative, matter-of-fact, nurturing, and occasionally fallible, but head of a community coping well in the modern world.

Similarly, Sayers's masterpiece, *Gaudy Night,* was about a college of women scholars whose solidarity and sensitivity defied their community's destruction and served their purpose of preserving culture and education. Observing these women, her protagonist Harriet Vane had a chance to reconsider her own life.

In comparing L'Engle and Sayers, it is intriguing to realize that their fame will probably be based on two popular genres: mysteries and children's books. Both categories represent a large proportion of mainstream literature, which paradoxically will allow these writers to continue to share their Christian beliefs with another generation. Such stories bring order out of chaos, good out of harm, while still dividing the world into good and evil.

Sayers and L'Engle say that easy answers are not available for the human condition because we must be fully human and forgive ourselves and others when we fail. For both writers the final touchstone for humanity is Jesus Christ, about whom Sayers commented that "[He] . . . never nagged at them, never flattered or coaxed or patronized, . . . took their questions and arguments seriously, never urged them to be feminine or jeered at them for being female . . . had no axe to grind and no uneasy male dignity to defend . . . [and] took them as he found them."[2] To which L'Engle adds thoughtfully that "we all fail each other . . . especially those we love most dearly. . . . but wasn't Jesus Christ singularly unsuccessful with a great many people?"

For Sayers and L'Engle it was finally their Christian belief in the independence of the creature—a maker made in the image of God who has the right to choose her way—that makes them hope-filled prophets for the next age. Instead of gazing sunstruck into the future or suffering millennium fever at the idea of a new creation, they offer an Anglican approach: to reexamine the recent past and learn from it as we carry forward traditions and continuities we will need in the next century—or tomorrow.

Author Biography

Alzina Stone Dale is a freelance writer/lecturer who has participated in conferences here and abroad. She has conducted workshops for the Newberry .Library's adult seminar program and has been an Urban Gateways' Artist in Residence with inner-city children. Her books include *Maker and Craftsman: The Story of Dorothy L. Sayers* (revised edition, Shaw, 1993), and *The Outline of Sanity: A Life of G. K. Chesterton* (Eerdmans, 1983), as well as a prize-winning series of mystery travel guides. Dale is a board member of Mystery Writers of America, the Ngaio Marsh Society, and the American Chesterton Society. She is also a member of the Authors' Guild, the Society of Midwest Authors, and the Dorothy L. Sayers Society.

Dale graduated from Swarthmore College in 1952 and received her M.A. in theology and literature from the University of Chicago Divinity School in 1957. An Episcopalian, she is married, has three children, and lives in the Victorian house where she grew up. Her ongoing ambition is to write Madeleine L'Engle's biography.

Madeleine L'Engle is for me a warm reminder that there is a sanctity in earthiness, a sublimity in the ordinary. I discovered her long before I met her. Upon first reading her books, I sensed a kind of awe—*Time Wrinkled*—and I felt a distinct wobble in this *Swiftly Tilting Planet*.

Years later we became friends. Though Madeleine has a lanky and unshrinkable charm, the near goddess dwindled at last into a real person. Her humanity soon became as overwhelming as her literary godhood once had been.

Since then I can brag about those wonderful quiet talks—rich with ordinary wisdom—that we have shared. Twice she has been in our home—helping with the dishes after dinner while we talked about Tolstoy surrendering his writing edge in late life to social causes. I think I am now as grateful for her friendship as for her literary clout.

Conversation never lacks a starting place with Madeleine and yet she is not chatty. She *listens* every person into the center of her counsel. She is grace that is never afraid of being awkward, and she is kindness that is never pushy. She is bright but never demands that anyone say so. Every cup of coffee is a kind of communion . . . every slice of toast, a banquet. I resent the thousand conversations we have never finished—I remember all of them. I treasure each of them.

Calvin Miller

13
In Favor of God

Calvin Miller

It was T. H. White's Guinevere who loved theology but never cared much for God. Why are we not surprised? Theologians sometimes love too much the God of footnotes and orthodoxy. Most of us, however, prefer to love God more than we love those who merely explain him. For most of us the God of theology is neither as personable nor as memorable as the God we discover in the bumps and thumps of the daily round. It is probably not theologians who best show us how to look for God in the grind. Maybe artists have been better at that. On this you may depend: wherever anyone hurts, some artist will be there painting the pain, sculpting the sorrow, writing up the irrational reasons of God. Madeleine L'Engle is an artist—a wordsmith with God on her mind.

Because of her books, Madeleine L'Engle was a friend to me before we ever met. But for the last twenty years we have become more direct friends. I could spend my chapter in this book rehearsing some wonderful moments in our relationship. But that sort of accounting can degenerate into boasting. So I would like to use my words to tell you why her worldview has so long supported my own. I will not be bookish about this. I am enough of a theologian to tell you precisely how Madeleine's Weltanschaung has undergirded my *Sitz im Leben*. But this would sin against Madeleine, who has an O'Keef-ish need to keep things simple.

My love for the craft of Madeleine L'Engle cannot be separated from her love of God. Her faith has three facets I find intriguing. First, she never tries to explain God, nor does she fear that her firm faith in God will be dislodged by reading those intellectuals who doubt or accuse God. She possesses a second quality that I find magnetic: to learn from those whose faith differs from hers she does not have to agree with them. A third commendation: she has used her decades to become acquainted with the world of ideas, never fearing that secular thinkers would erode her understanding of God. Her interest in the sciences and philosophy and theology and literature rewards her readers with a simple integration of life's ill-fitting ideas.

We never know what we believe while we only study our faith; we find this out by how we find ourselves acting when our beliefs must walk through fire. It is after such trials that we can legitimately name ourselves believers. It does little good to protest that we are Christians while we are only hearing sermons or reading our prayer books. It must be true, therefore, that writers write best not what they think about but what they have lived through. Madeleine L'Engle is plainspoken, to whomever she is speaking—whether God or his children. Her pilgrimage has sometimes caused her to hurt, and in the hurt, she always speaks very plainly to God. She even argues with him sometimes, but she never ignores him.

Although I have read Madeleine L'Engle for decades, it was not until recent years that I really came to appreciate her largess of Spirit. Following the illness and death of her life-long lover, husband, friend, and fellow artist, Hugh Franklin, a new laboratory dimension of life was added to her theories of faith. In that harsh laboratory her life theories all checked out, but she discovered a great truth: somewhere every ideology we hold authenticates itself only after it has run the gauntlet. It is in the trials, where the walls teeter and crumble, that we at last discern how real the foundations were.

Further, she understands that faith is the hidden agenda of life's darker times: God comes to us in the hurt. She also understands that in life pain often follows close upon the heels of ecstasy. But these random visitations of joy are what make it possible to bear the pain. The real lesson in these visitations of ecstasy and pain is that we were all created to be finely tuned receivers. We would receive more from God than we do if we did not create our own static, but the pain helps us remember that we constantly need to renew our relationship with God.[1]

With such a philosophy any writer is constantly being renewed by an unending series of rendezvous with God. And this kind of continual renewal sharpens the writer's craft. Thus, as both a believer and an artist, Madeleine L'Engle is in favor of God.

But what kind of God? He must be a God of grace and mercy above all. It is important for Madeleine to be sure that God should be always seen as the God of love. She can stand the idea that God is not always at hand when she feels a need for him. But she could not tolerate a God who enjoyed villainies of any sort. Forced to choose, she would rather have a God who is helpless than one who is bloody.[2] Nor would we ever serve a God who was ignorant of how he made us or what the future would be. We can only base our lives on God's knowing.[3]

Madeleine believes in God as the logical necessity of life. There are only three rationales by which we can live. First, we can live life as though life itself is all a cosmic accident. Second, we can live life as though there is a creator who made it all, and us all, but then set it to whirring without any real continuing interest in what he made. Third, we may come to believe that there is a personal and loving power behind the universe, and that each of us does matter to him. It is because he loves us so much that our lives have meaning.[4] One cannot doubt that the warmth of Madeleine's art proceeds from her view that love with a capital L is at the center of the universe.

I can sum up her view of God under four very simple ideas. Madeleine believes that God should be big, worshiped, the source of true art, and the Father of the Christ. Her view of God is dynamic by virtue of its simplicity.

God Should Be Big

> I am convinced that not only is our planet ultimately to be freed from bondage to Satan, but with it the whole universe—all the singing, dancing suns and galaxies—will one day join unhindered in the great and joyous festival.[5]

One can sense in L'Engle as in C. S. Lewis that God sometimes bears the brunt of our accusations. Job is the role model for all who demand that God should be big enough to be argued with. Even doubted.[6] L'Engle reminds us that God is big enough to be doubted and still exist. And when we brag that we never doubt, we may soon feel that we fully understand God. And once we feel that we really understand God, we are at least his peers if not his keepers. No, for L'Engle God is too big to be understood. She agrees with Augustine who said, "If you think you understand, it isn't God."[7] Because the Almighty is so vast in his love and inspiration, we are all free to live by the "Glorious Impossibles of God."[8] In L'Engle's words, this is the overwhelming proof of his greatness:

My faith in a loving Creator of the galaxies, so loving that the very hairs of my head are counted, is stronger than my work in life, and often is the work that pulls me back from faithlessness. . . . A man whose name is unknown to me, but whose words I copied out years ago, wrote, "God must be very great to have created a world which carries so many arguments against his existence."[9]

When God is seen truly, as his rightful size, the miracles are no obstacle to reason. Those who have the most trouble accepting the biblical miracles are those who confine God in the small cages of possibility. The universe itself is God's, as are all the laws that make the universe work. Therefore, why can't miracles happen? Why can't "love alter any law which Love demands"?[10] Neither the biblical miracles, nor all of creation, should be problems to those who see God in his true dimension. Madeleine feels a kind of pity for all of those who feel that they have to choose between God and evolution as a way of explaining how things have come to be. "The only question worth asking," she replies, "is whether or not the universe is God's. If the answer is YES! then why get so excited about the *how?*"[11]

It goes without saying that a big God would inspire big Christians with a spirit of largess. L'Engle expresses only disappointment with those whose sense of judgment betrays the size of their God. Little people who find time to be critical of others have a small "god" with no divine importance. "When religion causes judgmentalism, suspicion and hate," she writes, "there is something wrong with religion. It has become dehumanizing, and therefore, it is bad religion, and we become, once more, a horror and a hissing and an everlasting reproach."[12] Some Christians appear to love slandering others for the sake of elevating themselves; too many are of a "witch-hunter's mentality," always reading books looking for heretical words so they can indict some writer or artist for being less Christian than those who are most Christian.[13] She sees these who are ever "smelling out" things that are un-Christian to be living in violation of that beatitude that blesses all who are judged or persecuted unfairly.[14]

Such malevolent Christians are evidence that the great things of God are always under attack by the world of the demonic. Madeleine's word for these demonic spirits is a word for the enemy which she draws from the Greek, *echthroi*. The Echthroi are always stalking good, making the whole sick, the entire partial, the holy eroded by the contaminated.[15]

For Madeleine L'Engle all things are bound up in the size of God. When he is big enough to absorb our doubts about him, and large enough to be responsible for both the creation of the universe and the miracles of Scripture, then of course he is large enough to be the pier that underlies our worldview.

God Should Be Worshiped

They asked the abbot Macarius, saying, "How ought we to pray?" and the old man said, "There is no need of much speaking in prayer, but often stretch out thy hands and say, 'Lord, as Thou wilt and as Thou knowest, have mercy upon me.' But if there is war in thy soul, add, 'Help me,' and because he knoweth what we have need of he showeth us his mercy.[16]

It is not possible to read L'Engle without sensing that we are reading a writer who is humbled by the knowledge that God is both within her and beyond her. It is the Spirit of God within her that causes her to worship the God beyond her. Worship should be from the heart; such authenticity makes worship acceptable to God. It should be both spontaneous and planned. Were she to vote, Madeleine would cast her vote in favor of that worship which is more liturgical. Such worship best meets her need to offer God the highest praise in the best language and euphony. Madeleine was married to a Southern Baptist who hailed from Tulsa, Oklahoma, whose faith she always respected. Still, she never gave up her love of liturgical worship. In terms of formal worship, however, she believes that God can be worshiped only with the excellence of poetry and high hymnody. Excellence in worship is all-important. She is not much taken by choral music that remains too "blood of the Lamby."[17] But all worship should derive directly from a life of faith. Madeleine betrays her love and respect for evangelical theology in one rather elemental way: she believes that faith which can believe all that is written—even that which seems impossible—is the faith that blesses dull worship with bright vitality. Finding her raison d'être in Carroll's classic, Madeleine confesses that she, like the White Queen, finds it

a good discipline to practice believing in as many as seven impossible things every morning before breakfast. How dull the world would be if we limited ourselves to the possible. The only God who seems to me to be worth believing in is impossible for mortal man to understand, and therefore he teaches us through the impossible.[18]

It is the very irrationality of faith that gives us power over a logical world. Nowhere is this irrational power more obvious than in the Incarnation. It is Christmas which hones the idea. So she writes in *The Irrational Season:*

This is the irrational season
When hope blooms bright and wild.
Had Mary been filled with reason
There'd have been no room for the child.[19]

The irrational power and splendor of all that God can do should form our basis for worship. Only a God who is big enough to elude our understanding is great enough for our adoration.

One thing Madeleine never tolerates: the fundamentalist tendency to preach a fear of hell in order to motivate faith. Hell and heaven may be real, but to come to faith to avoid fire is to approach faith with too little love. Madeleine understands that too often we are motivated to worship a God of terror: such faith represents only a flight from fear, not an acceptance of redeeming love. Such fearful faith seeks to placate God out of fear of his wrath rather than out of joy for what he has done for us in Christ. Madeleine, after a tour of Egypt, noted that the old Egyptians worshiped two kinds of idols. One kind were cobras and crocodiles, gods but deadly enemies, whom the Egyptians hoped to placate with worship. But the Egyptians also worshiped the baboons. These baboons held the highest favor along the Nile because they were noticed to applaud the coming of the sun every morning. Madeleine definitely feels that joy and praise are the proper offerings of Christian worship. We are to worship Jesus not to keep him from throwing us into hell but because of the salvation he has provided us.[20]

The question that may be most vital for most Christians is, What do we see God to be? Are we determined to protect God from all who would attack him with doubt or outright atheism? "When we try to protect God," she says, "all we do is to stop our understanding of God from growing and deepening, because if we are open to new discoveries in the world within or without, it might change our comfortable image of God."[21] God must be big enough to elude us at times or he would never remain large enough to receive our true worship. She speaks of that worship in a hymn of her own:

Come, Lord Jesus, quickly come
In your fearful innocence.
We fumble in the far spent night
Far from lovers, friends, and home;
Come in your naked, newborn might.
Come, Lord Jesus, quickly come;
My heart withers in your absence.[22]

Alas, the final state of all who will not worship God is a withered heart. Madeleine is quite fond of the worship of the beasts and elders in the Apocalypse. Their final cry of "worthy is the Lamb" expresses the worship of her heart as well.[23]

God, the Source of True Art

You never enjoy the world aright, till the sea itself floweth in your veins, till you are clothed with the heavens, and crowned with the stars; and perceive yourself to be the sole heir of the whole world . . . till you can sing and rejoice and delight in God, and in good as coming from God.

Thomas Traherne[24]

No writer of the twentieth century better defines what it means to be a Christian artist than Madeleine L'Engle. She is convinced that all people are born artists, but most of them have their imagination fettered as they grow older.[25] What is it that corrupts the artistic spirit in most of the race? The loss of wonder. The perception and enjoyment of beauty gets displaced by what Thomas Traherne called the "dirty devices" of maturity. Madeleine does not spell these out, but all artists know what they are: imposed agendas, the tyranny of the urgent, the enforced prejudices of the status quo, the idea that art is financially unprofitable. She confesses, "A lot of my adult life has been spent in trying to overcome this corruption."[26]

Not only does God create us all to be artists, but Christian artists believe that their particular gift of art has come from God. Madeleine affirms that her gift has come from God, and she does her best to be a good steward of the gift.[27] Even the trials that come upon the artist do not come to consume the gift but to refine it. The artist is to see the fire as a refiner's fire.[28] All artists, like Mary of Nazareth, should say yes to the stewardship of these gifts. "What would have happened to Mary," L'Engle writes, "if she had said No to the angel?. . . She was obedient, and the artist, too, must be obedient to the command of the work."[29]

The arts, like God, are enduring through the ages. Madeleine confesses that she lives by this credo, which she once copied into her *Goody Book:*

> In the face of such shape and weight of present misfortune, the voice of the individual artist may seem perhaps of no more consequence than the whirring of a cricket in the grass, but the arts do live continuously, and they live literally by faith; their names and their shapes and their uses and their basic meanings survive unchanged in all that matter through times of interruption, diminishment, neglect; they outlive governments and creeds and societies, even the very civilizations that produced them. They cannot be destroyed altogether because they represent the substance of faith, and the only reality. They are what we find when the ruins are cleared away. And even the smallest and most incomplete offering at this time can be a proud act in the defense of that faith.[30]

In such a wonderful way Madeleine counsels the artist against diminishing her self-importance.

Still, if the gift has come from God, it should render the artist incapable of excessive arrogance about her talent. Artists can get a little lippy. One of Madeleine's students once commented that the only good artist is a dead one. The student went on to say that all artists should be shot after they have finished producing, for if they live on they will soon start commenting on their work and will spoil the product with too much appraisal. Beethoven, once complimented for one of his works, was asked what the piece meant. Instead of commenting, he simply sat down and played it again.[31]

And what of Beethoven's art? Where did he get it? What is its nature? Madeleine insists that all art is religious.[32]

The Christ at the Center of the Christian Artist

"Trumpets! Lightnings! The earth trembles! But into the Virgin's womb thou didst descend with noiseless tread."

And again, "No longer do the Magi bring presents to Fire and Sun, for this child made Sun and Fire."

This is a story so incredible that the world has tried to tame it, but it cannot be tamed, and we, like the Magi, are called to observe, contemplate, stand there, bring our gifts, and offer them. At our best, our offerings make us more human. . . .

Two thousand years ago Jesus came and called people to be more human, to pull us back to the Image in which we were created.[33]

Madeleine, here and there, has been criticized for her theology by those, as she pointed out, who are always smelling out heretics. Yet, even a surface reading of her works will find her consistently high in her view of God or Christ. Still, it is her view of Christ that marks her as far more than a casual believer. I find it hard not to be a worshiper myself whenever Madeleine speaks of Jesus. There is always a hint of the rhapsodic in her references to Christ. She refers to Christ's coming as "the birth of Love's most lovely Word."[34] "Jesus was lavish in all his ways," says Madeleine, a state of heart which she believes he modeled for the race.[35] She seems to me to sing her doctrine of Christ—"Let there be no question: I believe in the resurrection of Jesus of Nazareth as Jesus the Christ, and the resurrection of the body of all creatures great and small, not the literal resurrection of this tired body, the broken self, but the body as it was meant to be. . . ."[36]

But nowhere do Madeleine's rhapsodies swell greater than when she approaches the season of the Incarnation. For years I have kept her Christmas meditations to guide me in my own. She cannot seemingly think of what Christmas really means without breaking into hymns whose Christology is impeccable.

He came, quietly impossible,
Out of a young girl's womb,
A love as amazingly marvelous
As his bursting from the tomb.

This child was fully human,
This child was wholly God.
The hands of All Love fashioned him
Of mortal flesh and bone and blood,

The ordinary so extraordinary
The stars shook in the sky
As the Lord of all the universe
Was born to live, to love, to die.

He came, quietly impossible;
Nothing will ever be the same:
Jesus the light of every heart—
The God we know by name.[37]

This argument is art, but it would cause any honest theologian—artistic or mundane—to breathe *amen*.

With such a lyrical Christology always in place, is there any real need to explore other evidences of her pictures of the Christ? One thing is for sure, Madeleine's Christ is not a cheap little baal of hurried speculation. He is the Christ of the high altar of the heart and is ever worthy of worship. It is the Incarnation which fascinates L'Engle. She cannot get away from it. She marvels at it from a score of vistas. She ever speaks of it with wonder. Calling God *Elself,* she sees the Incarnation as the most extraordinary outpouring of love that can be imagined. She is lost to explain—as are all of us—that God could so love this sorry planet as to pay it a redemptive visit.[38] This kind of thinking about the Incarnation leads Madeleine to affirm the doctrine of the Virgin Birth: "If the Virgin Birth is taken away, isn't Jesus' Godness taken away too?"[39]

But for Madeleine, Jesus is not merely divinity on earth. He becomes for her the very definition of what it means to be truly human. He came for us *as* us.[40] His humanity was to encourage us in our trek through mortality. As she lived through her husband's terminal illness, she often read through the twenty-second Psalm. She exulted over Jesus' cross cry: "My God, my God, why hast thou forsaken me?" She experienced Christ as her companion in difficulty and said, "I am grateful that Jesus cried out those words, for it means that I need never fear to cry them out myself."[41] But Jesus is more than just a role model for how to go about being human; he wants to encourage this kind of true humanity in all who follow him. Madeleine wonders why Christians are so afraid to display their humanity—as though it were some sort of depravity. To need each other, to be human, ought to be *the* valued characteristic in the church. "Jesus came to us as a truly human being, to show us how to be human, and we were so afraid of this humanness that we crucified it, thinking it could be killed," she counsels. "And today we are still afraid to be human . . . which in some cases can lead to a complete moral breakdown. We are not perfect. Only God is perfect and God does not ask us to be perfect; God asks us to be human."[42]

Madeleine sees the Christ as the great Redeemer who reaches to save all who will come to him. Her view of grace draws its all-inclusive majesty from this little excerpt from *Crime and Punishment*:

> Then Christ will say to us, "Come you as well, Come drunkards, come weaklings, come forth ye children of shame". . . And he will hold out his hands to us and we shall fall down before him . . . and we shall weep . . . and we shall understand all things! . . . Lord, thy kingdom come.[43]

Madeleine's Faith

> The only God worth believing in does not cause the tragedies but lovingly comes into the anguish with us.[44]

Madeleine's writings are extensive, and I have read almost all of them. I have extracted this overview of her faith out of only eight or ten. I have included none of her novels, but all of them are built on views consistent with those I have cited. In past years Madeleine and I have often visited together and have always spoken of our faith in Christ. But I conclude this chapter where I began it. My esteem for Madeleine during the dark days of Hugh's passing have convinced me of her fidelity to God as much as any of her books. During those hard times, she never stopped praying, and while her prayers longed for answers that she often did not receive, the prayers themselves were the victory. During the depths of her crisis she asked, "What about prayer? Surely the prayers that have sustained me, are sustaining me. Perhaps there will be unexpected answers to these prayers, answers I may not be aware of for years. But they are not wasted. They are not lost. I do not know where they have gone, but I believe that God holds them, hand outstretched to receive them like precious pearls."[45] Madeleine never stops talking with God. To be sure, she questions, even bristles in the presence of the Almighty. But she never stops talking. How well she has won the right to say, "To ask is to be human . . . to continue to ask is to move into maturity."[46]

The years and the suffering have only strengthened Madeleine's hold on her gloriously impossible God— "How can I believe in a God who cares about individual lives on one small and unimportant planet? I don't know. I just don't know. But I cannot turn away from the hope and the mystery which never can be understood."[47]

As might be expected, the Easter Alleluias came slow for Madeleine after Hugh's death.[48] And yet she confesses that she still felt the breath of God, likening herself—to use Hildegard of Bingen's phrase—to "a feather on the breath of God."[49] But her later reflections show her grief giving way to the same affirmation her life has always exhibited. Madeleine began her journey into night with the words, "My husband is ill and I do not know how it is all going to end. Of course we never do."[50]

But this dynamic artist and believer continues to live out her view of final hope according to something she said many years before her darker days of struggle. But the wounded sing best, and Madeleine's life makes the point that when poets live through need, the world is blessed by their songs—songs that they themselves never quite understood while they were singing. One thing is for sure; Madeleine is right when she says, "It is only in the high language of poetry that anything can be said about God."[51] God stands out ahead of us. Madeleine's long and distinguished pilgrimage holds yet one great and final anticipation of God. And perhaps with this marvelous affirmation my brief appreciation of a dear friend should close, letting her own words describe her faith:

> And I am convinced that not only is our planet ultimately to be freed from bondage to Satan, but with it the whole universe—all the singing, dancing suns and stars and galaxies—will one day join unhindered in the great and joyous festival. The glorious triumph of Easter will encompass the whole of God's handiwork. The praise for the primal goodness of God's creation in the beginning will be rounded out with final worship, as John has expressed it in the Revelation: "Worthy art thou our Lord and God . . . To him who sits upon the throne and to the Lamb be blessing and honour and glory and might for ever and ever. Amen!"[52]

Author Biography

Calvin Miller is the author of dozens of books, including *The Singer* trilogy, *The Taste of Joy, The Empowered Communicator, A Covenant for All Seasons, The Book of Jesus,* and, most recently, *An Owner's Manual for the Unfinished Soul.* After serving in pastorates in Nebraska for thirty years, he joined the faculty at Southwestern Baptist Theological Seminary in Fort Worth, Texas, in 1991. Currently he is professor of communication and ministry studies and writer in residence at the seminary.

My first meeting with Madeleine, my awareness of her writing, came by means of my daughter Jennifer when she was a child. I noticed she was reading book after book written by one Madeleine L'Engle, and when I noticed Madeleine was coming to speak at Wheaton College, where I am on faculty, I asked Jennifer if she would like to meet her. Her astounded question jarred me into seeing what an amazing connection this writer had made with her. *"My* Madeleine L'Engle?" she asked in wonderment.

Since that day I have become a reader of Madeleine L'Engle and have rarely missed an opportunity to hear her forthright and insightful talks during her visits to Wheaton. Often I have been heartened and energized by her warmth and encouragement to me as a fellow writer she only meets *en passant* and yet remembers as a friend. In my fiction writing classes at Wheaton, I frequently cite her total commitment to writing, as well as her honesty and willingness to address the whole range of human experience in her writing—a powerful example to any aspiring writer. The joyful sense of transcendence, of "a world of radiant wildness where we see brilliance in the forests of the night" that pervades so much of her writing continues to delight and deeply inspire my life as professor, writer, and Christian woman.

Myrna R. Grant

14
The Celtic Vision

Myrna R. Grant

The rich and singular beauty of Celtic Christian art is presently attracting a revival of interest in the Celtic church. The luminous works of the Christian artists, poets, musicians, and writers of ancient Britain speak with surprising freshness and often astonishing paradox. The art and theology of these ancient Christians is both practical and imaginative, creative and disciplined, mystical and realistic.

Our age functions within a technological complex unimaginable to past generations. Contemporary science has triumphed over many of humankind's historical limitations of distance, time, and space. The Internet allows us access to potential millions of people across the world. Jet travel speeds us through distances only envisioned spiritually by Celtic poets. If we choose, we can shift the cycles of life, laboring all night, eating at all hours; if we like, we can be instantly diverted by the flick of a switch on a stereo, television, or computer. Our science has invented cures, transplanted organs, explored inner, outer, and subatomic space.

Yet we are sometimes disconcerted with society's ominous vulnerability. As simple a phenomenon as an electrical storm can plummet us into sudden helplessness. We have no lights. Television is silenced. Refrigeration and air conditioning are halted. Heating systems fail. Telephones are knocked out. Computer screens are blank and stores close. Traffic lights are dark and transportation systems grind to a complete stop. Only when the mighty engines of technology are restored are we flung back into our complex networks of progress and efficiency. We can be unsettled by the brief reminder that a universe of stillness and depth exists beyond our everyday reality of modern life. Perhaps an unspoken unease with technology, a sense that we have lost touch with our unique humanity, draws large and responsive audiences to the Celtic Christian arts of the distant past.

A central theme of Celtic Christianity is the presence of the spiritual world beyond and within outward appearances. The Celts saw the seemingly solid world as ever unstable, a site open to the supernatural, pressed upon by the world beyond, the shimmer of the eternal almost and often breaking through. The Celts called Earth "the third dwelling place," the fleeting abode of humans in a Christian triad of earth, heaven, and hell. They held that the visible worlds of nature and human nature were scrims through which the nearness of spiritual beings could ever be seen.

The saints of the four seasons,
I long to pray to them,
May they save me from torments,
The saints of the whole year!

The saints of the glorious springtime,
May they be with me
By the will
Of God's fosterling.

The saints of the dry summer,
About them is my poetic frenzy,
That I may come from this land
To Jesus, son of Mary.

The saints of the beautiful autumn,
I call upon a company not unharmonious,
That they may draw near to me,
With Mary and Michael.

The saints of the winter I pray to,
May they be with me against the throng of demons,
Around Jesus of the mansions,
The Spirit holy, heavenly.[1]

Celtic Christianity flourished in Britain from the fifth to the seventh centuries. While Europe was descending into a dark and pagan age of conflict and division after the fall of the Roman Empire, Celtic Britain was on fire with the Christian gospel. Thousands upon thousands of simple Celtic men and women became monks and missionaries, ablaze with the love of Christ.[2]

The first evangelists to Britain were Roman merchants and soldiers who carried the gospel with them to what was a remote outpost of the Roman Empire. Christian artifacts have been found in England dating from the late second century. By the late fourth century, when the great Celtic saint, Patrick, was born in what is now England, the Christian faith had taken root. At the age of sixteen, Patrick was kidnaped by a band of marauding Irishmen and taken to Ireland where he was sold as a slave. There he was converted to Christianity, and at age twenty-two he managed to escape to France where he subsequently was ordained as a priest. In 431 he was ordained as bishop of the Irish and returned to Ireland, the land of his captivity, as a missionary. Of his ministry in Ireland, Patrick wrote,

It would be tedious to relate all my labors in detail, or even in part; what matters is that God often forgave my stupidity and carelessness, and took pity on me thousands and thousands of times. There were many who tried to prevent my mission, saying, "What is this fellow up to, talking to God's enemies?" They were not being malicious, but were unhappy that a man so uneducated as I am should conduct such a mission. But though I am untalented, I have done my best always to be honest and sincere, with Christian and heathen alike.

I have baptized many thousands of people, but never asked as much as a halfpenny in return . . . I have traveled in the remotest regions of the country, where no Christian has ever been before, and there I have baptized and confirmed people, and ordained priests, and I have done so with a joyful heart and tireless spirit. I have given presents to kings and persuaded them to release slaves . . . I and my companions have at times been arrested and put in irons, and our captors have been eager to kill us, yet the Lord has always set us free.[3]

A famous Celtic "Breastplate" prayer for protection is attributed to Patrick.

I rise today
   in power's strength, invoking the Trinity,
   believing in threeness
   confessing oneness,
   of creation's Creator . . .

I rise today
   in heaven's might,
   in sun's brightness,
   in moon's radiance,
   in fire's glory,

in lightening's quickness,
in wind's swiftness,
in sea's depth,
in earth's stability
in rock's fixity

I rise today
with the power of God to pilot me.[4]

Sixty years after Patrick's death, another monk, later to become St. Columba, was born in county Donnegal, Ireland. Columba was highly educated and greatly gifted as an artist, poet, writer, and preacher. After years of successful though often controversial ministry, he sailed from Ireland to evangelize the pagan Picts in the wild and isolated highlands of Scotland. Accompanied by twelve disciples, he became "a wanderer for Christ" in the tradition of the Irish pilgrim-exile. The Old Irish term, *ailithre cen tintud*, "other-landness without return" gives a sense of his lifelong exile from his homeland. One of his poems describes his journey from Ireland to the Scottish coast:

Great is the speed of my coracle, its stern turned
*   upon Derry.*
Great is the grief in my heart, my face set upon Alba.
My coracle sings on the waves yet my eyes are filled
*   with tears.*
I know God blows me east, yet my heart pulls me west.
My eyes shall never again feast on the beauty of
*   Eire's shore.*
My ears shall never again hear the cries of her tiny
*   babes. . . .*
In Alba their hearts are hard, their tempers jealous
*   and harsh*
Their bodies plagued with disease, their clothes thin
*   and scanty. . . .*

*My heart is broken in two for love of my beautiful
    land.
If death should suddenly take me, the cause is grief
    for my home. . . .
Carry westwards my blessing to Eire carry my love.
Yet carry also my blessing east to the shores of
    Alba.*[5]

Columba landed on the tiny island of Iona on the west
coast of Scotland where even today Celtic high crosses,
striking in their execution and settings, give witness to
the wealth of symbolism found in Celtic Christian art.
Celtic artists used drawing compasses and complex grids
to create running patterns of curves and spirals to give
their art a flow of life and movement. They adapted
pagan motifs of plants, snakes, wolves, cats, fantastical
animals, and heavenly bodies into Christian themes and
images. The profusion of their creativity avoided repetition and the obvious. They loved ambiguity; shapes
often implied several meanings, changing and disappearing. There was a premium on originality and variety.
Through their genius they created intricate and sophisticated Christian motifs for chalices, bells, crosses, reli-
quaries, and Scripture manuscripts.

The Celts had a preference for memory over writing.
Although monasteries became celebrated centers of
learning, what was important to them was the inward
and spiritual possession of wisdom, which a person does
not forget. They also celebrated the development of
memory because of its intimacy with imagination. In
spite of their proclivity for visual and oral communication, writings of great literary and artistic value survive,
including biographies, epics of missionary voyages, and
most significant of all, devotional poetry and prayers that
give eloquent witness to their religious genius in the
use of the arts in worship. The Celts esteemed poetry
as the only adequate medium for the highest of human

spiritual expression,[6] even though poetry was an imperfect instrument.

Almighty Creator, it is you who have made
the land and the sea . . .
The world cannot comprehend in song bright and
 melodious,
even though the grass and trees should sing,
all your wonders, O true Lord!

The Father created the world by a miracle;
it is difficult to express its measure.
Letters cannot contain it, letters cannot comprehend it.

Jesus created for the hosts of Christendom,
with miracles when he came,
resurrection through his nature.

He who made the wonder of the world,
will save us, has saved us.
It is not too great a toil to praise the Trinity . . .

Purely, humbly, in skillful verse,
I should love to give praise to the Trinity,
according to the greatness of his power . . .[7]

Celtic theology, depicted in its art, poetry, and music, held that humankind was in bondage to profoundly malevolent spiritual forces that operate in the world and in the human spirit. Humans need to be rescued from these powers. The exuberance of Celtic art expresses the joy of Christian deliverance. Christ releases this holy and beautiful world from its captivity to evil; darkness is scattered and light shines forth, freeing humans, body and soul, from the shadows that lie across creation.

By far the most influential writing for the Celtic

church was the Bible. It was the foundation for the education of the young and the inspiration for poets, artists, and song writers. They took for granted that the Bible was God's word and counsel and should be understood and obeyed by all. This Celtic stress on biblical studies and devotion created an indifference to pagan authors and even to early church commentaries. Their art reflects a literal understanding of Scripture; they did not engage in discussion, speculation, and definition. Obedience was central.

Their doctrine of God was Trinitarian. God was eternal, without beginning or end, omniscient and worthy to be adored. The supreme authority of God to discipline his people was often noted, but only in correction, not punishment or anger. The great love of Christ in taking human nature to die for fallen humankind was a very frequent theme, although the virgin birth was neither mentioned nor suppressed. The resurrection of Christ was often alluded to and the Holy Spirit was seen to have spoken by the prophets and to be the agent that inspires saving faith. The Celts, like the Eastern church, held that the Holy Spirit proceeded from Christ alone. A study of God revealed qualities of benevolence working toward the salvation of fallen humankind.

I praise the threefold
Trinity as God.
Who is one and three,
A single power in unity,
His attributes a single mystery,
One God to praise.
Great King I praise you,
Great your glory.
Your praise is true;
Poetry's welfare
Is in Elohim's care.

Hail to you O Christ,
Father, Son
And Holy Ghost, Our Adonai.

I praise two
Who is one and two
Who is truly three,
To doubt him is not easy
Who made fruit and flowing water
And all variety,
God is his name as two,
Godly his words
God is his name as three,
Godly his power,
God is his name as one,
The God of Paul, and Anthony . . .[8]

The Celtic appreciation of nature flowed from the conviction that the natural world was created by the word of Christ and revealed the character of God. This confidence produced beautiful mystic nature poetry.

Let us adore the Lord,
Maker of marvellous works,
Bright heaven with its angels,
And on earth the white-waved sea.[9]

The literal interpretation of Genesis produced the doctrine that humans are created with a body, a soul, and a spirit. Humans are mortal, and after punishment, the sinner would be annihilated; humans are immortal only on condition of their obedience to God's law. The Ten Commandments were of great importance in Celtic theology, and generally, Old Testament rules were followed. Christians obey God's commandments by means of God's grace. The theological controversies of the Mediterranean countries were unknown to the Celts, or when known, were of little interest. The will of God for them was plainly revealed in the totality of Scripture.

Anyone who rejects God's will
Is like a leaking ship on a stormy sea,
Is like an eagle caught in a trap,
Is like an apple tree which never blossoms.

Anyone who obeys God's will
Is like the golden rays of the summer sun,
Is like a silver chalice overflowing with wine,
Is like a beautiful bride ready for love. [10]

Salvation was achieved only by the merits of Christ, which were imputed by the Savior to the believer. Humans are helpless to save themselves and only by divine grace can any good be accomplished on earth. Also in accord with Eastern theology, Celtic Christians did not believe that Adam's fall infected humankind with original sin. They believed that each individual sins through the example of Adam and through the exercise of personal choice. When an individual chooses Christ, that person is freely justified by God and will be resurrected to eternal life.

I rise with you, dear Jesus, and you rise with me.
As the oil of gladness pours upon you, it trickles
onto me.
As the fire of love burns within you, it warms my
heart.
As the breath of eternal life fills your body, I know
that I shall live forever,
As the word of God comes from your lips, your
name is written on my forehead.
As you reach out to bless mankind, I feel your
embrace drawing me close.
I rise with you, dear Jesus, and you rise with me. [11]

Celtic Christian traditions were based on the conviction that all Christians were competent to interpret Scripture for themselves. They made no distinction between ethics and morality: any belief or practice thought to be at variance with Scripture was summarily rejected. In accordance with the Old Testament, they were Sabbath keepers, with everyday activities ceasing from sundown on Friday to sunset on Saturday. Communal worship services were in the vernacular and were for worship and most importantly, instruction—the preaching simple and practical, with the Lord's Supper celebrated with bread and wine. Celtic clergy could marry, and women themselves exercised the highest ecclesiastical functions, presiding over monastic communities. The monastery founded by St. Brigid, renowned for her care of the poor and the sick, became the largest monastic community in Ireland. "Brigid's Feast" reflects her legendary generosity:

I should like a great lake of finest ale
For the King of kings.
I should like a table of the choicest food
For the family of heaven.
Let the ale be made from the fruits of faith
And the food be forgiving love,

I should welcome the poor to my feast,
For they are God's children.
I should welcome the sick to my feast,
For they are God's joy.
Let the poor sit with Jesus at the highest place,
And the sick dance with the angels.

God bless the poor,
God bless the sick,
And bless our human race.
God bless our food,

God bless our drink,
All homes, O God, embrace.[12]

For the Christian artist—fifth-century Celtic mystic or almost-twenty-first-century Westerner—to suggest, to evoke, to explore something of the transcendence of creation, the astonishment of redemption, the grandeur of God, which "flames out, gathers to greatness," the vision that in nature lives the "dearest freshness of deep down things"[13] remains the high creative task and deep joy. This is powerfully captured in Madeleine's many writings and in the following poem:

Whether I kneel or stand or sit in prayer
I am not caught in time nor held in space,
But thrust beyond this posture, I am where
Time and eternity are face to face;
Infinity and space meet in this place
Where crossbar and upright hold the One
In agony and in all Love's embrace.
The power in helplessness which was begun
When all the brilliance of the flaming sun
Contained itself in the small confines of a child
Now comes to me in this small action done
In mystery. Break time, break space, O wild
and lovely power. Break me: thus I am dead,
Am resurrected now in wine and bread.[14]

Author Biography

Myrna R. Grant has been a faculty member of the Communications Department of Wheaton College for the past twenty years. She teaches fiction writing, screen writing, and media analysis. Her own writings include the best-selling classic, *Vanya*, the Ivan series of young people's novels, *The Journey,* a biography of Rose Warmer, and other books, scripts, and scholarly writings. Her most recent publication, *Poems for a Good and Happy Life* (Doubleday, 1997), is an anthology of poetry celebrating the seven cardinal virtues. She frequently lectures on writing and communication in workshops and seminars in Western and Eastern Europe and has been a Visiting Fellow at Edinburgh University and a Visiting Scholar at Oxford University.

I wrote Madeleine a decade ago and said that I wished to take her for my model, that my own patience and kindness among the public be enriched. Such women as this are the saints of their age, and the age is mean indeed if it does not recognize them.

Walter Wangerin, Jr.

15
Madeleine, My Eli

Walter Wangerin, Jr.

"Oh dear Walt," Madeleine L'Engle wrote in a letter she sent me more than a decade ago: "I'm not a very great model. I, too, fail both in spirit and in attitude and sometimes plain fatigue, and I suspect that's always part of the human predicament."

I do not doubt the truth of her statement, neither that it is true nor that she experiences it as the truth. Nevertheless, by a gentle irony it is that very truth which frames the equal truth of her genuine, rich kindness.

And that the woman should in her letter remember the failures more easily than the successes of her kindness is Madeleine L'Engle's gracious and unself-conscious humility.

Which, precisely, I have determined to praise out loud. There are few enough saints in our universe—and fewer still who maintain sanctity while burdened by celebrity. Then let us bless the few while they are, before they are not and cannot benefit of blessing.

In her disclaimer Madeleine was responding to a precarious letter of my own, in which I had tried to define my admiration for her, the public person.

Writers are called to write: to write well, to write accurately, to write affectingly, to write with craft and the heart's persuasion. *Writing* is their vocation. It is enough that they spend their greatest attentions on this private activity. It is, for many of us, more than enough—so that we have already spent the full account of our energies when, next, we must go out among the public. Responding in person to people in the public square was not in the writer's job description. And, past weariness, some of us simply lack the graces necessary to honor hungry and demanding fans.

I am myself swiftly depleted of merciful kindness. And I hate it that I am. Exhaustion and clumsiness can make dangerous mistakes—and I fear I leave wounds or confusion behind when I rush from the public square back to my writer's den.

But Madeleine L'Engle!

I have always marveled at her patient ability to meet crowds of individuals all *as* individuals. She shows such goodness of spirit, she practices such precious particular attention, that after all there are no crowds where she is—though a writer of her stature and consistent output could always avoid the masses by the righteous argument of deadlines and the greater efficiency (the "greater" labor) of publication. She is neither cynical nor hypocritical: her general fame is an easy chair from which she genuinely loves to love people, one by one.

So I wrote her to say that I was taking her as my model, and did she mind? I was praying that one day my own self-absorbed and cranky spirit would expand to fulfill the sweet ministry I saw in her, not just as a writer writing well, but as a servant of the hearts of people, and so of God.

And she wrote back, "Oh dear Walt, I'm not a very great model."

Her modesty is sincere. But her assertion is wrong. And

I am right. Such women as this are the saints of their age, and the age is mean indeed if it does not recognize them.

"For the word of the Lord was rare in those days, and there was no frequent vision." And the child Samuel, who ministered unto the Lord before Eli, could be forgiven if, when the Lord called him by name, he thought he heard his mentor speaking.

Eli was a good man, after all. He represented God to the child. He was himself faithful unto the Lord. And the deepest measure of his faithfulness was that he could in blessed humility direct Samuel away from himself to the Lord whom they both served.

> And it came to pass at that time, when Eli was laid down in his place, and his eyes began to wax dim, ere the lamp of God went out in the temple of the Lord, and Samuel too was laid down to sleep, that the Lord called Samuel and he answered, "Here am I." He ran to Eli and said, "Here am I, for thou calledst me."

Thousands of thousands of readers know Madeleine L'Engle as the canny, perennial author. She has published something near a half hundred books for children and adults, a remarkable number of which remain in print.

Hundreds of thousands of audience folk know Madeleine as a Lincolnian lecturer, earthily rough-hewn in mood and humor and human observation, absolutely accurate regarding her craft, and ethereal in matters of the spirit. She is a tireless traveler, impartial in the selection of her venues.

But I add to that knowledge this wonder: The public personality and the private person are the same. This woman wears no mask to please a paying multitude. The temperate, insightful, affectionate, galactic, and homely L'Engle whom we meet in the book—that *is*

L'Engle. The vastly interested Madeleine, the literate Madeleine, the devout and faithful, the votive and the homiletic Madeleine—these are all the same she who shuffles between bedroom and kitchen at Crosswicks. The quick-witted and personable woman at the podium: Madeleine L'Engle. She.

And she is Eli of Shiloh.

And I am the child, Samuel, hearing in her voice *bath qol,* "the daughter of the voice" of God.

> "Here am I, for thou calledst me."
> But he said, "I called thee not. Lie down again."
> And he went and lay down again.
> And the Lord called yet again, "Samuel."
> And Samuel arose and went to Eli and said, "Here am I, for thou didst call me."

I first met Madeleine in the autumn of 1986. If there ever was a time when she had indisputable reason to excuse herself from new people and new relationships, that was the time.

Colorado. The weather was cold and growing colder. As night drew darkness like a garment over the mountains, it began to snow. We were a group of authors gathering together for the first time, all of us aware of the others in print, but many of us having never met face to face before. In vans we traveled from the airport to a tiny mountain resort. The drive was long and cramped. Yet the instant she met us, she smiled and talked.

There was in her no evidence that anything had any a greater command of her attentions than my wife and I. She permitted our minor topics a major weight in her life.

As we stood in a hallway waiting for dinner, Thanne said, "You taught our son to read."

"Did I?" Madeleine beamed, immediately pleased. Tall

woman, close-cut hair, a wide face with eyelids of mush-room flesh, a dress like drapery: she was regal before us. But she reached and touched Thanne's shoulder, inviting intimacies. "Did I, really?"

"Matthew," Thanne said. "When he was young, he could not contain himself. Wild child, too much explo-sive energy to sit still and learn things less physical, like words and symbols and reading and stories.

"But when we began to read *A Wrinkle in Time* to the children, Matthew's imagination found a whole, huge world in which to run and fight and laugh and dwell. Oh, Madeleine, the book was so important to Matthew that he began to read the rest of the series on his own. He *learned* to read. And he learned how to use language himself."

Madeleine's face chased Thanne's story, as if *she* were Matthew, the child of passionate energy. She suffered, fleetingly, the news of Matthew's hyperactivity. She smiled to hear of his marvelous quietude while reading her books. And she grinned like a split melon at the triumph of his mind thereby. Easily she embraced Thanne and hugged her and became a full and instant friend, in love with Matthew, rejoicing with Matthew's parents.

No, there was no evidence of distractions or difficul-ties in Madeleine's life. We, when we spoke to her, were the whole of her world in that moment.

The poet Luci Shaw was with us that week.

Her husband Harold had died some months earlier, and she had translated her grief into a remarkable manu-script entitled *God in the Dark*.

There came an afternoon when Luci, sitting erect in a wicker chair, began to read from her journal of per-sonal loss. I was at first impressed by the sibilant, civil clarity of her pronunciation. Next, the value of her words and the great weight of their sorrow moved me. As Luci read, I grew quieter and quiet in my spirit.

But suddenly I realized something of infinite depth: Luci was reading for Madeleine's sake. One woman was granting the other a sacred companionship. Deep was calling unto deep and together they attended to the mysteries—for Madeleine's husband, too, had died. But recently! Hugh, her spouse of forty years, had scant weeks ago left Crosswicks for heaven's distant home.

So I was, that afternoon, granted the privilege of witnessing the friendship of these two women, each one bearing the other's spirit one sphere higher, softly, softly, in strong sorority.

So, more wonderful than that, I understood an even greater gift: that Madeleine's appreciation of our son's success was bequeathed to us while she was mourning her husband's departure! In spite of her personal sorrow, this woman honored the child she had never met, and she blessed his parents with gladness.

This is the selflessness of the saints. *Deo gratias!* I cry.

This is the kindness of those who serve not their own flatteries or fortunes, but the Lord, the God of us all.

This is the holy humility of the good-est and faithful-est servants.

For I wrote Madeleine a decade ago and said that I wished to take her for my model, that my own patience and kindness among the public be enriched.

But she wrote back—my dear and lasting friend wrote back—and,

perceiving that it was the Lord that had called the child, said, "Go, lie down, and it shall be, if he call thee, that thou shalt say, 'Speak, Lord, for thy servant heareth.'"

So Samuel went and lay down in his place.

And the Lord came and stood and called as at other times, "Samuel, Samuel."

Then Samuel answered, "Speak, for thy servant heareth."

In this wise shall I continue to honor the saintly Madeleine L'Engle, even as I find in her—in her manner and in her soul—the presence of the Lord, unto whom she has directed me, and whose shall all my greater service be.

But *Eli* means no more nor less than *my God.*

And *Madeleine* derives from *Magdalene,* who was among the foremost disciples of Jesus.

Author Biography

Walter Wangerin, Jr., first came into prominence as the award-winning author of *The Book of the Dun Cow.* He has since won many awards and honors for his books, which include *The Book of God, Miz Lil and the Chronicles of Grace, Ragman and Other Cries of Faith,* and *The Manger Is Empty.* Among his children's books are *Probity Jones and the Fear Not Angel, Thistle, Potter,* and *Branta and the Golden Stone.* He also wrote *Crying for a Vision.* Wangerin lives in Valparaiso, Indiana, where he holds the Jochum Chair at Valparaiso University and is writer in residence.

My friendship with Madeleine L'Engle has been a great grace, as I describe in the following essay. As we celebrate her eighty years of living, let us give thanks for the longevity of her forebears!

Barbara Braver

16
The Journey of Becoming

Barbara Braver

It would be interesting to know how many writers' workshops Madeleine L'Engle has conducted over the years—how many volumes of words she has coaxed forth from both seasoned and aspiring writers. In a certain sense, their efforts are a tribute to her generous spirit, and we can celebrate the achievements of the writers she has encouraged, even as we celebrate her own life and work.

Year after year eager new groups of writers have met with Madeleine—in university classrooms, in parish halls, at retreat centers, and in her own comfortable living room. Others have met her only on the printed page. I have no idea of their number, and I suspect Madeleine has not either. This I do know: Madeleine's own writing and her teaching about writing encourage and nurture other writers as they struggle to put pen to paper. Before meeting Madeleine, many who have drunk thirstily from her well thought of themselves as merely scribblers in secret, possibly to no good purpose. With encouragement, they discovered they had within them stories waiting to be told, treasures to be excavated.

From Madeleine's own words we know she is unself-conscious during the act of writing. "When the work takes over, then the artist is enabled to get out of the way, not to interfere. When the work takes over, then the artist listens," she has written.

The thinking has come before the writing. Sometimes it happens like this. One minute she is with you in her kitchen, her sharp knife flashing through a mound of garlic. The next minute, though her hands continue their efforts, her mind is miles away, in another place, communing with her characters perhaps, devising a plot or outlining a chapter.

Then, each day, every day, she allows the work to take over as she listens, sitting silent with her yellow pad on her lap, or coming, faithful, to the computer as if to a romantic rendezvous. She listens, gets out of the way, and the words come. And after, after the writing, she spends concentrated hours revising her manuscripts with precise, calligraphic, markings.

Though Madeleine has disciplined herself to unself-consciousness while writing, she is demonstrably able to articulate her interaction with the creative process. She offers a rare gift when she describes the fearsome act of letting go to creativity and "riding the wind," as she calls it, in ways that embolden others to follow. Through the liberal offerings of herself, Madeleine goes far beyond imparting the rules of her craft. At a deeper level, she is a companion and fellow pilgrim, willing to walk with you as you do the hard work of stringing one word after another, telling stories, making meaning, and most of all, becoming your truest self—the one God intends you to become.

To my joy, since the beginning of our friendship, Madeleine and I have traveled together on the road to becoming. We met some fifteen years ago when a magazine assigned me to do a profile of her. Over the next years, we corresponded and kept, as she says, "in telephonic communication." In the late 1980s, when I took a job that required me to leave home and husband to spend several nights each week in New York City, frequent dinners with Madeleine were a happy compensation. Then, when her granddaughters both finished graduate school and moved from her large apartment to their own spaces, and I was in the process of rethinking my New York living situation, Madeleine invited me to be her "housemate." These past years have been a delight, as we have laughed quite a lot (often in incredible irreverence), cried a great deal less, tucked into marvelous dinners at the end of long days (she cooks, I clean up), relished our oatmeal and coffee on chilly mornings, prayed together, and generally enjoyed the extraordinary blessings, ever available, in the seemingly ordinary events of our lives.

Words have been my close companions since before I could spell or make my hand form anything looking like a letter. I started a newspaper when I was ten years old and named it *Neighborhood News*. A cat funeral is the only major story I remember. But then, not much happened during the placid 1950s in the semi-rural community of my growing up days. The paper lasted for the early part of one summer, coming out weekly. I wrote the copy longhand and pecked it out, letter by letter, on my Uncle Jim's ancient Underwood, which probably was not all that old at the time. Even now I can feel the bite of their silver rims as I carefully depressed the round keys. I thought it all quite magical.

My collaborator and friend, Susan Stanley, and I sold our few copies—each originally typed in those days before ready photocopies—to our neighbors, who had known us *in utero* and were no doubt amazed at our persistence.

My next experience of the writing life began a summer or two later when another girlhood friend, Martha Taylor, and I would sneak out of our respective houses at first light in search of dew-soaked grass and poetic inspiration. Martha's dog usually smelled adventure and trailed along. The only line I remember still, with a wince, was inspired by that solid little black dog: "Bucky is my dog, my own." In the poem, I changed his name from Zachary to preserve his anonymity when I became famous.

In spite of these early experiences, and my formal education in English and journalism, I did not easily come to name myself a *writer*. Since I hung up my waitress apron after a summer between college years, I have never made a cent for doing anything except writing or editing, in one form or another. Even so, writers were not me: they were Shakespeare or Milton or Blake or Louisa May Alcott or E. B. White or Barbara Pym, for heaven's sake. So, when I honor Madeleine's ministry of encouragement, and the coaxing forth of words, I speak from personal experience. I hope, perhaps, that I may speak as well for others to whom she has given courage to ride the wind.

In honor of what Madeleine has done to encourage and inspire writers, and all who yearn to claim themselves as such, in these next pages I offer poems of *becoming*. I have included among them several sonnets because that form has been important to Madeleine since she began writing sonnets sometime in her teen years. Within the strict form, she found freedom. In *A Circle of Quiet* she describes the sonnet as "the perfect analogy of the structure which liberates."

My own sense is that the sonnet form not only provides a discipline within which to be free, but that in working out the rhyme, I find what is true for me and uncover feelings previously unavailable to me in my conscious mind.

In *A Wrinkle in Time*, one of Madeleine's wise characters, Mrs Whatsit, compares our lives to a sonnet: a strict form, but freedom within it. As Mrs Whatsit says: "You're given the form, but you have to write the sonnet yourself. What you say is completely up to you."

And is it not so for writers, to our fear and unspeakable delight? "What you say is completely up to you."

Inspiration

It serves the work to halt my searching
    flight,
the restless circling of the outer quest,
and thus find what is seen with inner sight,
when body, mind, and spirit come to rest.

But quietness is not my usual way,
and lesser cares have fouled my inner
    place,
as louder voices hold soft ones at bay
and weeds choke off my path to sacred
    space.

My task is first to tug out every weed,
to silence errant voices that intrude,
eliminate those forces that impede,
and wait on Spirit-muse like lover wooed.

And when I have enacted my small part,
I wait for gifts of words to fill my heart.

No poetry

For days, weeks, no poetry.
No message wells up
from my truest being.

Perhaps I have not gone down,
to meet her
   in the soul place.

Have I merely greeted her in passing
an acquaintance
  worthy of only a careless wave?

Or is she the current patient
on my examining table
  to whom I give focused attention
    over a narrow range?

No meetings these.
How then, to meet her?

Since you ask, she will show you:
  in the terrors of the night
  in the beauty of the morning;
  in bread broken, where she is at one
    with all that is,
    seen and unseen.

Find her thus.
Attend to the moment,
  full of grace.
Strike the rock
  and watch the water gush,
    living

The Sabbatical Sonnets

I. Sabbatical

The pages tempt me with their unmarked
    space
these summer months when I can simply
    be
and wander through the wilds of inner
    place
allowing soul and body to float free.

Still I must look for guides along the way
some bread crumbs on the path to finding
     me
or into brambles and dark voids I'd stray
and from the pregnant silence I might flee.

This time of God's is given as a gift
and God will cast those crumbs for me to
     find
God's purpose will emerge through
     focused drift
as false bonds loosen and the truer bind.

I say good-bye for now to safe routine
to search in faith for futures dimly seen.

II. The reckoning

I sing a song of summer that has fled
and find my song begins as a lament
for hours and days that from my store
     were bled
for time now gone and possibly misspent.

As fall returns so does the inner court
to stand in judgment on my use of time
They say that they can give no good
     report
on fits and starts and efforts worth one
     dime.

"Shut up," I shout. "Stand down. You are
     dismissed.
You have no sense of who or what I am.
Your words to me I'll consciously resist
and for your judgment I don't give a
     damn."

This holy time was God's own gift to me.
Of my return we'll have to wait and see.

III. The resolution

Were I to take a measure of these days
I'd ask myself about my faithfulness.
I'd ponder if I've found some truer way
and tended to God's leading more—or less.

Am I now more who I am meant to be?
Have I made progress on the pilgrim's road?
Can I some further growth expect to see
from bulbs I planted and from seeds I
sowed?

I dare to ask these questions, then I wait
for I myself the answers do not know.
As only God's own Spirit knows my fate,
I pray that towards God's vision I might
grow.

Content for now to be a lump of clay
as in the potter's loving hands I stay.

"Because I am a story teller, I live by words. . . . Stories are
able to help us become more whole, to be named."[1]

The words inside me

The words inside me
bump against each other
and abrade my soft interior.

They gather,
a teasing chorus,

pose mute,
and then
at some secret signal
hurl themselves
against the drawn curtain
of my consciousness.

By day,
they drop,
insensible,
and litter my unplowed field
like so many cowpies
carelessly dropped
until walking is dangerous.

At night,
I awaken to their frolic,
too late,
and watch them go
leaving only silvery trails,
evanescent.

At first light,
I open wide
to let them out
and they vaporize
against a still background
to gather strength
for another rush.

I've come to know them now
and so will lay my plan
that they might stay
tamed, somewhat,
and sign,
at least,
my guest book.

The Inventory

When King Henry died,
a scant 55 years—
  though who would believe it
  given his marital history,
  and the swells and creases
    of his swollen girth—
a commission was appointed
to measure, count, and catalogue
his worldly goods,
  from the crown that weighted his regal
    head
  to the collar that fit round the neck
    of his favorite hound.

The inventory of his possessions
fills four substantial volumes
kept for historians
and the merely curious
at the British Museum
  the material history of a life
  in small detail,
    the worn pillows, frayed curtains,
    cutlery, cups, and clothing,
    and one mottled leather eyeglass case,
  the detritus of his earthly days.

And what of me, at a greater age,
my accumulations, accretions?
When I die, who will count each pillow
  and note its wear?
The attic horde could fill one book,
  things left behind, at each chapter's end:
    a button-eyed doll,
    yellowing silks of baptisms
      and a wedding

skates grown dull
letters crumbling
and broken chairs,
rump-sprung.
What could they tell of me,
and my mortal life?

Little enough, I think.
I have not saved with history in mind.

Better to find a living witness
who wrote down stories
remembers laughter
noted sins, and counted blessings
remarked on warm hands
measured longing, and joy
one who knew me
as I was.

Better to find a true witness
and leave my possessions,
unnumbered, unrecorded,
trusting,
rather,
in a living word.

The prodigal heart

I've never learned frugality of heart
to hoard and store against a lonely day
to measure love and keep the greater part
to nurture only those I knew could pay.

Heedless I've loved without regard to
cost.
I've spent myself and not learned how to
save.

I have not kept a tab on what I've lost
or balance sheet on what I got or gave.

So is my heart now emptied out and poor
and rendered barren by my spendthrift
*   way?*
Must I now look for bargains that are
*   sure,*
for profit and a guarantee of pay?

Oh no: I've learned that one plus one
*   makes ten*
as all I've spent comes back to me again.

Remembering

We are made, they say,
by what we remember
and choose to forget.
Our memories are our treasure
as well, Pandora's Box.
Within them is the sacred mystery of all life,
of who we are,
and how we came to be.

We release them like ghosts
from long-sealed tombs.
The stone rolls back and out comes
Lazarus, perhaps, smelling like death
or the shade of our mother.

Wanting more
we excavate our plot of time passed
like archaeologists
fingering carefully through the rubble.
Old bowls, broken as promises.
Cloth, woven to last.

And we wait.
Sometimes we simply wait
for snowdrops
who withstood cold and the frost of many
winters
and now, improbably, emerge.

And so it is.
We find our memories
or they find us
and attach themselves
like extra appendages.

Better to search, I say
to find what wants to be found
and, of course, what prefers
to remain
hidden.

Author Biography

At various times, Barbara Braver has been a technical editor, a small town newspaper reporter and copy editor, the director of communications for the Episcopal Diocese of Massachusetts, a freelance writer, a poet, and the information officer for the national Episcopal Church. She lives in Gloucester, Massachusetts, where she spends what time she can looking at the light.

Notes

1 The Partnership of Art & Spirituality

[1] Luci Shaw, *Polishing the Petoskey Stone* (Wheaton: Shaw, 1990) 227.

[2] George Herbert, *Poems*.

[3] Walter Brueggeman, *Finally Comes the Poet: Daring Speech for Proclamation* (Minneapolis: Fortress, 1990).

[4] Madeleine L'Engle, *Walking on Water* (Wheaton: Shaw, 1980) 161.

[5] Alfred Corn, ed., *Incarnation* (New York: Viking Penguin, 1990) 25-26.

[6] Revelation 1:11, 17, 19

[7] Matthew 13:16

[8] Dorothy Sayers, *Gaudy Night* (New York: HarperCollins, 1936) 186.

[9] Luci Shaw, *Writing the River* (Colorado Springs: Piñon, 1994) 36.

4 Looking for Truth in the Age of Information

[1] For this summary of information theory I am indebted throughout to Jeremy Campbell's *Grammatical Man* (New York: Simon & Schuster, 1982), an excellent treatment of both the theory and some of its implications.

[2] Malcolm Browne, "Scientists See a Loophole in the Fatal Law of Physics," *New York Times* 29 May 1979: C1, C4.

[3] Psalm 139:13, 15-16

[4] John 1:1-3

5 Gospel Quartet

[1] Robert Lowell, *Lord Weary's Castle and The Mills of the Kavanaughs* (New York: Harcourt, Brace & World, 1951) 63.

[2] Eugen Rosenstock-Huessy, *The Fruit of Lips,* ed. Marion Davis Battles (Pittsburgh: Pickwick, 1978) 23.

[3] Rosenstock-Huessy 24.

[4] Reynolds Price, *Three Gospels* (New York: Scribner's, 1996) 37.

[5] Hoskyns and Davey, *The Riddle of the New Testament* (London: Faber & Faber, 1931) 137ff.

[6] Alfred Corn, ed., *Incarnation: Contemporary Writers on the New Testament* (New York: Viking, 1990) 2.

[7] "He takes up a phrase or a word, plays with it, repeats it, turns it inside out, then drops it and revolves in a similar way round another, very often one that has been thrown up in the process of handling the first. We have to come to terms with this and accept it, otherwise we are simply baffled and irritated by his refusal to make his points and advance in an orderly manner." Austin Farrer, *A Rebirth of Images* (Westminster: Dacre, 1949) 26.

[8] Edward Dahlberg, *Can These Bones Live?* (Ann Arbor: U of Michigan P, 1967) 25.

[9] William Temple, *Readings in St. John's Gospel* (London: Macmillan, 1959) xvii.

[10] Robert Browning, *The Poems and Plays of Robert Browning* (New York: Modern Library, 1934) 301.

[11] John Calvin, *Calvin's Commentaries 5 (Ezekiel, Daniel)* (Grand Rapids: Associated Publishers, n.d.) 7.

[12] Early on the images were assigned in various orders. Eventually, Augustine's scheme prevailed: Matthew the Lion, Mark the Man, Luke the Calf, and John the Eagle. Henry Barclay Swete, *The Gospel According to St. Mark* (London: Macmillan, 1908) xxxviii. Walther Zimmerli, *Ezekiel I* (Philadelphia: Fortress, 1979) 126.

[13] J. Massyngberde Ford, *Revelation* (Garden City, NY: Doubleday, 1975) 76.

[14] Gershom Scholem, *Major Trends in Jewish Mysticism* (New York: Schocken, 1946) 79.

[15] Dating in these matters is imprecise, but there is some consensus that "this mysticism may have been practiced in esoteric circles in the time of the second temple, probably during the first centuries BC and AD." Ford, *Revelation* 79.

6 *Taking the Bible Seriously*

[1] Northrop Frye, *The Great Code* (New York: Harvest/HBJ, 1982) 33.

[2] Michio Kaku, *Hyperspace* (New York: Anchor, 1994) 3.

[3] Joseph Campbell, *The Inner Reaches of Outer Space* (New York: Harper & Row, 1988) 18.

[4] Song of Songs 4:1-4

[5] Frye 84.

[6] Exodus 15:11

[7] Genesis 8:21

[8] Isaiah 44:6

[9] Amos 8:4-6

[10] Amos 5:21-24

[11] Hosea 11:1-4, 8-9

[12] Isaiah 53:2-6

[13] Isaiah 49:6

[14] Luke 4:16-21

[15] Frye 231.

[16] Frye 132.

8 The Incarnation and Poets-Priests

[1] Sallie McFague, *Speaking in Parables* (Philadelphia: Fortress, 1975) 15-16.

[2] John Bunyan, *The Pilgrim's Progress* (New York: New American Library, 1964) 12.

[3] Bunyan 12.

[4] John Milton, *Complete Poems and Major Prose* (New York: Odyssey, 1957) lines 564-66, 568-73.

[5] Richard B. Hughes, "George Herbert and the Incarnation," *Cithara* 4 (1964): 24.

[6] Hughes 23.

[7] C. A. Patrides, ed., *The English Poems of George Herbert* (London: Dent, 1974) 14-15.

[8] Patrides 192.

[9] Thomas P. Roche, ed., *Essays by Rosemond Tuve. Spencer. Herbert. Milton* (Princeton: Princeton UP, 1970) 175.

[10] Mary Ellen Rickey, *Utmost Art* (Lexington: U of Kentucky P, 1966) 173.

[11] Patrides 61.

[12] W. H. Gardner and N. H. Mackenzie, eds., *The Complete Poems of Gerard Manley Hopkins* (London: Oxford UP, 1967) 100.

[13] Paul L. Mariani, *A Commentary on the Complete Poems of Gerard Manley Hopkins* (Ithaca, NY: Cornell UP, 1970) 91.

[14] Gardner & Mackenzie 66.

[15] Gardner & Mackenzie 66.

[16] Gardner & Mackenzie 69.

[17] Donald McChesney, *A Hopkins Commentary* (New York: New York UP, 1968) 66.

[18] Gardner & Mackenzie 69.

[19] McFague 104.

[20] Gardner & Mackenzie 53.

10 The Joyous Turn

[1] David Steindl-Rast, "Paths of Obedience: Fairy Tales and the Monk's Way," journal article, date and source unknown.

[2] Walter Wangerin, Jr., "Hans Christian Andersen: Shaping the Child's Universe," *The Classics We've Read, and the Difference They've Made,* ed. Philip Yancey (New York: McCracken, 1993) 9.

[3] Madeleine L'Engle has often told interviewers (I was one of them) that she does not write "for children." When I interviewed her for *Catholic Twin Circle,* soon after publication of *The Sphinx at Dawn,* I pressed the point. Her response was: "I write for children when what I have to say is too difficult for adults."

[4] J. R. R. Tolkien, "On Fairy-Stories," *Essays Presented to Charles Williams,* ed. C. S. Lewis (Grand Rapids: Eerdmans, 1966) 38-89.

[5] Madeleine L'Engle, *Walking on Water: Reflections on Faith and Art* (Wheaton: Shaw, 1980) 138-139.

[6] Geoff Ryman, *Was* (New York: Penguin, 1992) 360.

[7] Ryman 361.

11 A Great Cloud of Witnesses

[1] Madeleine L'Engle, *A Circle of Quiet* (San Francisco: Harper & Row, 1980) 62-63.

[2] Madeleine L'Engle, *A Ring of Endless Light* (New York: Farrar, Straus & Giroux, 1980) 321.

[3] Madeleine L'Engle, *A Wind in the Door* (New York: Farrar, Straus & Giroux, 1973) 178.

[4] George Woods, "The State of the Field in Contemporary Chil-

dren's Fantasy: An Interview with George Woods," *Lion and the Unicorn* 1.2 (1977): 5-6.

[5] Madeleine L'Engle, *An Acceptable Time* (New York: Farrar, Straus & Giroux, 1989) 282.

[6] L'Engle, *An Acceptable Time* 304.

[7] Madeleine L'Engle, *Walking on Water: Reflections on Faith and Art* (Wheaton: Shaw, 1980) 122.

12 The Lives of the Saints

[1] Alzina Stone Dale, "L'Engle and Sayers, the Artist as Model," *The Episcopalian* May 1983: 12.

[2] Dorothy L. Sayers, *Are Women Human?* (Grand Rapids: Eerdmans, 1971) 47.

13 In Favor of God

[1] Madeleine L'Engle, *And It Was Good* (Wheaton: Shaw, 1983) 126.

[2] Madeleine L'Engle, *Sold into Egypt* (Wheaton: Shaw, 1989) 76.

[3] L'Engle, *Sold into Egypt* 65.

[4] Madeleine L'Engle, *A Circle of Quiet* (New York: Seabury, 1979) 63-64.

[5] L'Engle, *And It Was Good* 209.

[6] L'Engle, *And It Was Good* 63.

[7] Madeleine L'Engle, *Walking on Water* (Wheaton: Shaw, 1980) 129.

[8] L'Engle, *Walking on Water* 105.

[9] L'Engle, *Walking on Water* 149.

[10] L'Engle, *Sold into Egypt* 207.

[11] L'Engle, *Sold into Egypt* 64.

[12] L'Engle, *Sold into Egypt* 98.

[13] L'Engle, *Sold into Egypt* 112.

[14] Madeleine L'Engle, *Two-Part Invention* (San Francisco: Harper & Row, 1988) 206.

[15] L'Engle, *Two-Part Invention* 206.

[16] L'Engle, *Two-Part Invention* 205-206.

[17] L'Engle, *A Circle of Quiet* 35.

[18] Madeleine L'Engle, *The Irrational Season* (New York: Farrar

Straus & Giroux, 1977) 19.

[19] L'Engle, *The Irrational Season* 27.

[20] Madeleine L'Engle, *A Stone for a Pillow* (Wheaton: Shaw, 1986) 169.

[21] L'Engle, *And It Was Good* 46.

[22] L'Engle, *The Irrational Season* 214.

[23] L'Engle, *And It Was Good* 209-210.

[24] L'Engle, *Sold into Egypt* 99.

[25] L'Engle, *Walking on Water* 51.

[26] L'Engle, *Walking on Water* 52.

[27] L'Engle, *Sold into Egypt* 112.

[28] L'Engle, *Two-Part Invention* 146.

[29] L'Engle, *Walking on Water* 22.

[30] L'Engle, *Two-Part Invention* 103-104.

[31] L'Engle, *A Circle of Quiet* 172.

[32] L'Engle, *A Circle of Quiet* 49.

[33] L'Engle, *Sold into Egypt* 97-98.

[34] L'Engle, *Sold into Egypt* 101.

[35] L'Engle, *Sold into Egypt* 163.

[36] L'Engle, *The Irrational Season* 108-109.

[37] L'Engle, *Sold into Egypt* 148-149.

[38] L'Engle, *Sold into Egypt* 58.

[39] L'Engle, *Sold into Egypt* 190.

[40] L'Engle, *Sold into Egypt* 58.

[41] L'Engle, *Two-Part Invention* 96.

[42] L'Engle, *Sold into Egypt* 20.

[43] L'Engle, *Walking on Water* 68-69.

[44] L'Engle, *Two-Part Invention* 172.

[45] L'Engle, *Two-Part Invention* 186-187.

[46] L'Engle, *Two-Part Invention* 188.

[47] L'Engle, *Two-Part Invention* 168.

[48] L'Engle, *Sold into Egypt* 121.

[49] L'Engle, *Two-Part Invention* 168.

[50] L'Engle, *Two-Part Invention* 77.

[51] L'Engle, *Two-Part Invention* 168.

[52] L'Engle, *And It Was Good* 209-210.

14 *The Celtic Vision*

[1] O. Davies & F. Bowie (Editors), *Celtic Christian Spirituality* (New York: Continuum, 1995) 39.

[2] R. Van de Weyer, *Celtic Fire* (New York: Doubleday, 1990) 1-2.

[3] Van de Weyer 32-33.

[4] Davies 41-42.

[5] Van de Weyer 60-61.

[6] J. Mackey, *An Introduction to Celtic Christianity* (Edinburgh: T & T Clark, 1989) 16.

[7] Davies 27.

[8] Davies 30-31.

[9] Davies 30.

[10] Van de Weyer 172.

[11] Van de Weyer 168-169.

[12] Van de Weyer 39-40.

[13] Gerard Manley Hopkins, "God's Grandeur," *Gerard Manley Hopkins,* ed. C. Phillips (New York: Oxford UP, 1995) 114.

[14] Madeleine L'Engle, *The Weather of the Heart* (Wheaton: Shaw, 1978) 80.

16 *The Journey of Becoming*

[1] Madeleine L'Engle, *Walking on Water: Reflections on Faith and Art* (Wheaton: Shaw, 1980) 37, 45.

Other Books in the **WHEATON LITERARY SERIES:**

The Weather of the Heart, poems by Madeleine L'Engle. Paper, 96
   pages.
WinterSong: Christmas Readings, by Madeleine L'Engle and Luci
   Shaw. Cloth, 208 pages.

Available from your local bookstore or from Harold Shaw Publishers,
Box 567, Wheaton, IL 60189. 1-800-SHAWPUB